Fisher

Starting to Race

Starting to Race

No. 1 in the Commodore Series

In the same series

Starting to Cruise by Guy Cole

JOHN FISHER

Starting to Race

(taking into account the 1965–68 official Racing Rules)

Adlard Coles Limited London 1967

Published by Adlard Coles Ltd. 1967
3 Upper James Street Golden Square London W1
Based on an earlier book by John Fisher of the same title and published by Adlard Coles Ltd. in the Bosun Series.

Printed in Great Britain by
Cox & Wyman Ltd, London, Fakenham and Reading

Contents

List of Plates

Plates 1–6 are by Eileen Ramsay, cover photo and plates 7 & 8 by J. B. Moore

Introduction

The *new* 'Starting to Race' is one and a half times the length of the book I wrote under the same title in 1959 and later revised. It has to be! So much has happened since then—new racing rules, new scoring methods, new techniques for starting races and sailing them, and new safety measures.

And the standard of Club racing has improved so much that even first year helmsmen reject the old haphazard happy-go-lucky attitudes that won races a few seasons ago.

So I have tried to include herewith the best of what's new and to leave out some of what most people now take for granted.

Here's to good planing!

1

The Lure of Racing

It might seem puzzling at first sight that reasonable people, who are free to take their boats out almost anywhere at random, prefer, instead, to race them round marks, and to do so at times laid down for them in advance.

In self-justification, a racing helmsman would probably protest that if, one week-end, he tried to go cruising instead of racing, he would spend the whole time worrying how to get back in time to go to the office on Monday. But this is only one reason and not the most important. In reality, a man of a certain type cannot help preferring racing to pottering aimlessly about from one harbour to the next. For example, if he is a perfectionist, and believes that a boat should be sailed perfectly or not at all, then he will want to race, in order to see just how close to perfection he is getting. If he is a thruster, he will welcome the miniature battles that take place not only in the van of the racing fleet but all the way down the line. If he is quick-witted he will enjoy having to make split-second decisions as he races for the starting line or rounds the mark.

For the sociable man or woman, racing means a club. It means sailing with friends with whom the race can be shared for some considerable time after it is over.

Above all, it means concentrated sailing. In a single afternoon's racing you can have more thrills than in a month's cruising. The dodging and feinting at the start, the near collisions, the excitement of having to make a forced gybe that you don't fancy at a mark...none of these occur outside racing.

There is tension because the boat is being sailed all out and because, in small boats in particular, you often have to carry more sail than you need on the beat in order to have a chance of planing on the reaches. You are continually taking calculated risks. That is, you keep standing on toward the shore until the last possible second if it helps you to keep out of the tide. You round the mark within a whisker touch if it's reasonably safe to do so and if it will help you to pick up a place on the next leg of the course.

A racing boat is designed differently from any other. It is the distinction between a polo pony and a pack-horse. If the adjectives 'Lively', 'Sensitive', 'Responsive' appeal to you, then you need a racing boat rather than a knock-about or family model.

I won't deny that a racing boat is feminine, and therefore a capricious creature. She wastes no time on reflection. She has no patience with anyone who misjudges her moods but, to those who understand, she can be a perfect partner. Let us begin by considering small boats, that is centre-board boats holding one or two people. This is, and should be, the field for people starting to race. It will be time enough later for them to think of ocean racing.

Most clubs organize races for at least two small boat classes, the choice depending partly on the resources of the members and partly on the weather, tidal conditions, depth of water, launching facilities and other local conditions.

As a first move towards taking up racing in the United Kingdom, one can hardly do better than join the Royal Yachting Association (Address: 5 Buckingham Gate, London, S W 1). This Association is the National Authority for yacht racing and publishes, amongst other useful information, a list of recognized yacht and sailing clubs with their addresses and in many cases the types of boats sailed by their members.

The RYA deals with almost everything affecting yachting in the UK and has more than 1,000 registered yacht clubs on its books. It administers some of the most important classes of racing yacht. It co-ordinates the fixtures proposed by clubs and classes into a balanced programme for each year, and it protects yachtsmen against unfavourable legislation of every kind whether by Ministries, Local Authorities or Harbour Boards.

It picks the yachtsmen who represent Britain in the Olympic Games and is the final board of appeal in protest cases involving incidents between racing yachts in the UK. In fact racing could hardly exist without the RYA. The Royal Yachting Association also publish a list of sailing schools of approved competence.

And here are two other useful addresses.

The Central Council of Physical Recreation, 6 Bedford Square, London, WC1, runs excellent lectures on dinghy racing and seamanship. But you should apply for tickets in advance.

Anyone interested in sailing on the nearest sand or gravel pit should find it useful to get in touch with the Information Department of the Sand and Gravel Association of Great Britain, at 48 Park Street, London, W1.

When it comes to choosing a boat the newcomer will probably do well to pick one belonging to one of the well-established classes rather than one for which he may not find a ready market when he wants to sell her. The expenses of the first season can be halved by sharing a boat. Sharing may also help to solve the problem of finding a crew and may give the new helmsman an insight into the class-racing technique. Alternatively, the would-be owner may prefer to spend a season as crew in someone else's boat or, perhaps, in several different classes of boat. The crew is usually offered a turn at the helm at the end of each race and so gets to know the boat from both ends, as it were.

There are three main types of racing boat. At one end of the scale are the one-design classes in which no variations are allowed in the hulls, construction, and rigging, and only the minor fittings may be varied. The advantage of a one-design class is that, since all boats are alike, the newer boats don't outdate the old, and the old antiques therefore keep their secondhand value in a highly satisfactory manner. Racing is close because all the boats in a class behave alike whatever the weather. The second main group of racing classes are known as Restricted Classes or Development Classes. In these, only the main dimensions—for example, length, beam, and sail area—are fixed, and the hull lines, construction, and other important items can be varied. Consequently many new and successful ideas are first tried out in restricted classes and there is none of the stagnation which can and often does affect vintage one-design classes. Finally there are the Formula Classes such as the 5.5 metre which are more read about than sailed in. In these, almost everything can be varied provided that you pay an appropriate forfeit. For instance you can give your boat extra stability provided that you decrease the sail area; or if you want more sail area, you can have it by giving up stability. The main stipulation is that the various dimensions, when related to one another in the manner laid down by the formula, shall not exceed the required limit of 5.5 metres, in the case of this class.

Some classes, besides controlling measurements, also limit the number of new sails and the frequency with which they can be replaced. In other classes the vessel cannot be taken out of the water and scraped or coated with anti-fouling paint more than a given number of times each season.

These regulations are made to cut down expense, and to see that the helmsman with the largest bank balance does not gain an unfair advantage.

One of the cheapest one-design boats for children is the Optimist which has achieved great popularity both in Scandinavia and the United States. The Optimist is a blunt-nosed beamy flat bottomed boat measuring 7ft 6 in × 3ft 8 in with a single small sail set up with the help of a light sprit or spar. It is designed to carry 110 lb of added buoyancy and can safely be sailed single-handed *in sheltered smooth water*. The Optimist Class Racing Association in Britain can be reached at Clouds Hill, Old Bursledon, Hants.

Other single-handed racing classes but for grown-ups include the 11-ft Moth, the 12-ft 4½-in Solo, the 13-ft 1½-in long OK dinghy, and of course the 14-ft 9-in Finn used for the single handed event in the Olympic Games.

The OK and the Finn are one-design classes. The Moth is a development class and several national variations of it are to be found.

Turning to boats that need a crew as well as a helmsman we have (for those under eighteen) the 10-ft 6-in Cadet which is far more advanced than the Optimist and carried a spinnaker as well as a mainsail and jib.

The Mirror, one of the cheapest dinghies designed for grown-ups, is only slightly larger than the Cadet and carries slightly less sail. In other words you won't find it too exacting.

One of the most popular of the one design racing dinghies is the National 12-ft Firefly with a nominal 90 sq ft of sail. This is made from laminated moulded wood and is easily handled and maintained. Slightly larger and more exacting is the National Enterprise, a double-chine boat of 13-ft 3-in length with 113 sq. ft of sail.

A selection of close on a hundred small boats and their

vital statistics is to be found in *Sailing Dinghies* and the general principles of sailing in *Starting to Sail* published by Adlard Coles Ltd.

I am often asked how much it costs to keep a racing boat, but am seldom able to give a very definite answer. Size comes into it of course, and an increase of a foot or two in the length of the hull makes a considerable difference to the bill at the end of each season. The locality is a factor too. If you are sailing from somewhere fashionable or from a place where labour has been snapped up by some new refinery, prices will be high. And vice versa.

A great deal depends on how much of the maintenance work is carried out by the yard and how much by the owner. The weather, too, has a big effect on the cost of racing. One can rightly expect a boat that is sailed inland on well-protected water to cost rather less to run that its fellow sailed in a choppy maritime estuary. Again, if the boat is kept on moorings and is therefore in constant motion, the wear and tear may be higher than it would be if she were kept ashore and under cover when not sailing. The more frequently a boat is raced the more replacements she is likely to need.

One way of finding out the running cost of a boat is to ask a trusted and fairly methodical owner in the class (any others are apt to forget to average what they spent in one year as compared with another).

Personally I have found that the upkeep of a 12-ft boat (excluding insurance and racing fees) works out at not much more than twenty cigarettes a day, which is a small price to pay for a season's fun.

It is possible in normal times to buy even a small racing dinghy on credit—either through a bank or a hire-purchase company. Buying a boat on credit sounds improvident but may save you money if prices are rising and may also give you an extra season's sailing. A Bank loan is usually cheaper (note that the banks charge interest only on the unpaid balance of the loan whereas a hire-purchase company works on a flat rate calculated on the original advance without taking account of instalments paid).

It is worth taking some care to make sure that you and your boat are fully insured. Waters these days are becoming more and more crowded and accidents more and more expensive. Damages for injury or loss of life *might* in an exceptional case run into thousands of pounds and it is all the more reassuring to know that the premium for insuring up to say £50,000 is relatively small. If buying a second-hand boat don't take it for granted that the unexpired insurance will cover you. Underwriters don't automatically continue the insurance of a boat that has passed to a new owner.

Marine insurance policies cover damage to your own vessel if she is stranded, sunk, burnt, or in collision but normally exclude racing unless extra cover is taken for this risk.

The policy will also take account of where the boat is to be sailed and how long she is to be laid up. So if you decide to start sailing earlier than you planned or to go on later, let the insurance company know. A vessel is not necessarily regarded as fully laid up if she is in the yard under repair because the risk of fire, etc., is greater than if she were put away under cover. Also tell the insurers if you are going to some open meeting outside the area specified in your policy. You will not normally be covered for clothes (or stop-watch) lost overboard unless these form part of the boat's permanent equipment.

Amounts recoverable for gear ashore may be limited to 15 per cent of the total insured value while the vessel is in commission or 33⅓ if the boat is laid up.

A comprehensive marine insurance policy should cover accidents caused by loading or unloading gear (your heavy metal centre-plate is dropped and makes a hole in the hull) malicious acts (small boys take out the drain plug so that the boat fills on the next high tide), contact with aircraft (not unlikely if you are rescued by helicopter) and theft of the vessel or fittings following forcible entry.

Underwriters do not usually object to the owner allowing his crew to steer the boat as long as he is in charge or to his lending it to an experienced helmsman but the boat must not be chartered without the insurer's written permission. A special policy may be needed if the boat is used for team-racing or, as in the case of a club boat, by a number of different helmsmen.

Finally extra insurance including third-party will be needed if the boat is towed behind a car. The trailer should be valued and insured separately.

1. A Mirror 16 planing during a race on the River Medway. Note the upright trim, the weight well aft and the stern wave left well behind.

2. The prototype of the new International Tempest Class sailing in the Solent with John Oakley at the helm.

2

A Medley of Races

The best known yacht races in the world are two-boat contests such as are sailed for the America's Cup. Best known, I said, but not, in practice, frequently met with. For if only two boats were allowed per race, what unemployment we should soon sec among the other club members!

Sailing would become very different too, because in two-boat matches the leading boat's course is often controlled by the following boat which she has to cover. For instance in a match race she has to spend a great deal of time obstructing the other boat from passing her to windward, a luxury she could not afford in an ordinary race for fear of a third boat getting ahead by another route.

We can take it, however, that most racing is in groups of from 5 to 105 boats. Such races can be either level or handicap. Most class races are sailed without handicap, although some clubs work a system by which a boat that wins a race incurs a handicap penalty in the next. Handicaps become unavoidable, however, when boats of different sizes and sail area race against each other, and for this purpose there are two main systems; (1) handicaps by time on time and (2) handicaps by time on distance.

In 'time on time' the allowance is calculated at so many minutes or seconds per hour of the elapsed time either of the leading boat or, more often, of the individual boat which is receiving the handicap.

Time on distance is calculated according to the length of the course.

Neither system works perfectly. For instance, if a race is sailed in light airs with periods of calm, the time on time system favours the slower type of yacht; for her time allowance over the larger boat increases while both are becalmed. In a time on distance race, on the other hand, you get no more allowance if the course is a dead beat against strong winds (requiring say 50 per cent more distance through the water) than you would if it were a straight run in fine weather the whole way.

Perhaps the decision about which system to use should depend on the type of weather to be expected during the race.

Many different systems have been invented for deciding what handicap, on time or distance, one boat should have against another. One very simple formula, which avoids higher mathematics and measuring difficulties, gives each boat a rating equivalent to half the sum of her length on the waterline and the square root of the sail area. This formula is generally known as the Seawanhaka Rule and is widely used in the United States.

There are nevertheless special difficulties in handicapping small boats fairly against each other in any given race.

For example in the case of a 12-footer, a knot or two extra wind-strength can mean the difference between reaching at say 4 knots and planing at possibly double that speed. So a handicap given to a 12-footer against a large quicker-planing boat might be good on one day and unfair on another. Even a change in the tide may affect planing because a weather-going tide, although it will increase the apparent force of the wind and therefore the sailing speed, may raise so much sea that the smaller boats are slowed more by it. So in theory the tide should be allowed for too when calculating the ideal handicap.

Furthermore, on any given day the weight of the crew in a small boat may be an advantage or an overwhelming handicap. In these circumstances the best that one can do is to average the performance of different well-known types of boat in competition with each other in all kinds of weather and work out a skeleton handicap system into which the lesser-known types of boat can be fitted.

This is the basis for the system first used by the Portsmouth Sailing and Racing Association and since administered by the Royal Yachting Association. The 'Portsmouth Rating' given to each class is normally printed in the *RYA Year Book* and can be supplied by them in pamphlet form. It can be used for handicapping either by time on time or for time on distance. The handicapper can avoid many head-splitting calculations by using the Langstone Tables worked out for the Portsmouth Association. These tables give each boat a conversion factor by which its actual finishing time is multiplied in order to find out the corrected finishing time on handicap. The Royal Ocean Racing Club handicap results are also worked out by a conversion factor system.

When organizing handicap races some clubs start all different sizes of boat together which adds to the excitement (and peril) at the start. Other clubs send the boats off at different times according to their handicaps in the hope that they will all finish at the same moment. If they are right this second 'pursuit race' method makes a better and safer spectacle.

Regatta day is the occasion for such specialities as ladies' race, crews' race, and races between yachts sailing from other clubs to take part in the regatta.

Two other kinds of racing remain to be described. The first is single-handed racing. This is sometimes carried out in boats with mainsail and jib, as in the International Ten

Square-Metre Canoe but more often in boats with one sail only, such as the Finn used in the Olympic Games, the OK dinghy, the Solo, sponsored by the *Yachting World* magazine, the Moth and various other types. Single-handed sailing is usually more strenuous and less sociable than normal racing. It requires a carefully planned lay-out within the boat and special tactics in order to compensate for the absence of a crew.

One of the main difficulties of single-handed racing is that there is so little of it, and unless you live in a place where it is already well established you may have to travel in order to find competition. Helmsmen in the Finn Class, where the standard is very high, go abroad regularly for international racing in order to keep in the front rank of the class.

There is probably an ideal weight for a helmsman who proposes to sail in any single-handed class, a point worth considering before entering the field. Not everyone is prepared to add artificially to his weight like the Olympic gold medallist Paul Elvstrom who cheerfully soaks his sweater in cold water before or during the race if he feels that he needs a few extra pounds of weight, and it might indeed sometimes be unseamanlike to do so.

Finally, there is team-racing, which many helmsmen pro-

---

1. Reef knot – a normal way of joining two ropes of equal thicknesses.
2. Round turn and two half-hitches – for making fast.
3. Figure-of-eight knot – to prevent a rope's end from running out through the block.
4. Rolling hitch – secures a rope to itself. The white knot will not slip down even when the fall of the white rope is strained downwards.
5. Bowline knot – the loop stays the same size even under strain.
6. Quick-release reef knot.
7. Sheet-bend – for holding the clew of a sail or the corner of a boat cover.

YACHTSMAN'S KNOTS

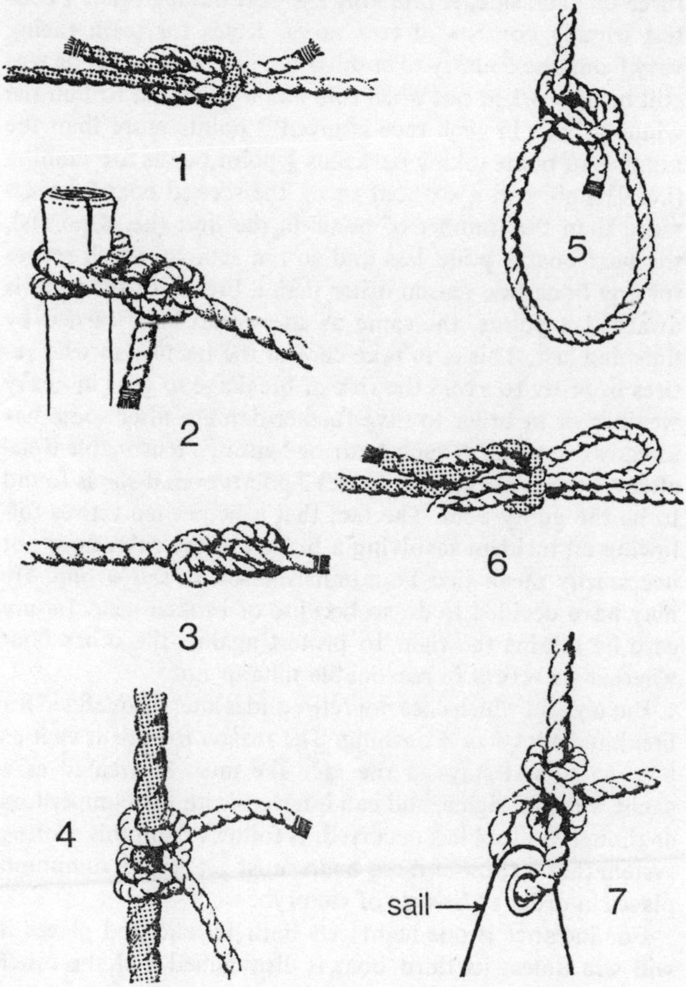

1

2

3

4

5

6

7

sail

claim as the most interesting form of all because one can be certain of sailing against hand-picked opposition. Six boats, three on each side, is probably the best number, and a contest usually consists of two races. Rules for team racing vary from one country to another (an international code was still being worked out when this was written). In Britain the winning boat in each race is given 3 points more than the number of boats taking part plus ¼-point bonus for winning (i.e. 9¼ points in a six-boat race), the second boat 2 points more than the number of boats in the fleet (i.e. 8 points), the next boat 1 point less and so on. A boat which retires for any bona-fide reason other than a breach of the rules is awarded 4 points, the same as she would have earned by finishing last. This is to take care of the helmsman who retires in order to avoid the risk of breakage to gear in heavy weather or in order to save further damage after some has already occurred. A yacht retiring 'within a reasonable time' after a breach of the rules scores 3 points even if she is found to be the guilty boat. The fact that a helmsman retires following an incident involving a breach of the rules does not necessarily mean that he admits himself in the wrong. He may have decided to do so because of broken gear. In any case he retains the right to protest against the other boat whether he retires in reasonable time or not.

But a yacht which does not retire and is later disqualified for breaking rules scores nothing. The reason for this is that as long as a boat stays in the race she must be treated as a yacht with full rights, and can interfere with her competitors as though no foul has occurred. It follows from this scoring system that a team of three boats must get certain minimum places in order to be sure of victory.

For instance if one team gets both 1st and 2nd places it will win unless its third boat is disqualified and the other side has no disqualification or retirement.

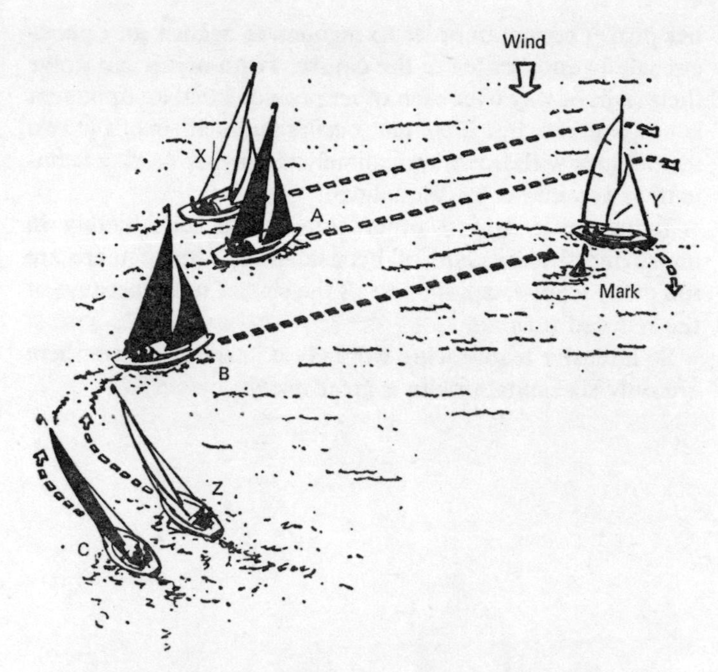

FIG. 2. Team racing tactics. 'A' holds off 'X' at the mark, thus forcing her to turn wide allowing 'A's team-mate 'B', to get through to challenge 'Y'.

If the team cannot manage to win 1st and 2nd places, it must try for 1st, 3rd and 6th or 1st, 4th and 5th or 2nd, 3rd and 5th. 'Legitimate interference' plays a much greater part in team-races than in ordinary contests. For instance if two teams, white sailed and coloured sailed, are sailing a team race and a white-sailed boat is well in the lead it may be better for a coloured-sailed boat (lying second) to concentrate on downing another competitor in order to let a team-mate through into second place than to pursue the leading white-sailed boat. But a yacht may not luff or bear away from her proper course in order to manœuvre against an opponent sailing another leg of the course. Team-mates can waive their right of way over each other provided that an opponent is not baulked, but if contact occurs and neither of the two team-mates withdraws immediately the higher scoring team-mate is automatically disqualified.

Team-racing against other clubs helps considerably in improving the standard of helmsmanship. But if there are too many team-races, the rest of the classes suffer because of the reduced turnout.

So intensive team-racing works best in classes where there are only six boats, or else a great many.

3

How a Race is Organized

A big class championship meeting with a hundred or more sails thrusting towards the starting line is a wonderful sight. But meetings like this take a lot of organizing. Imagine the staff work required for one day. You may be doing it yourself.

As early as possible the host club sends out a preliminary notice of their big fixture, giving the date of the meeting, the rules under which it will be sailed, the date and time of each race, together with entry forms showing the entry fee and the closing date for entries.

In the meantime, posters advertising the meeting will have been sent to clubs likely to be interested, at least six weeks before the closing date for entries. Two weeks before the racing begins, those who have entered must be told the time and place at which they will get the sailing instructions and the detailed racing programme. In the case of a national championship the host club also provides a list of hotel accommodation, etcetera, for helmsmen and crew, and a map showing the parks for dinghies, trailers, and cars.

Organizing a dinghy park is no easy matter. You need enough space for the boats to be rolled over for hull-polishing and someone has to mark out the berths at the correct angle so that when a boat is rolled over, her mast will clear her neighbour's. Fresh water and hoses will be wanted for washing down the boats and a supply of hay bags or old motor tyres for resting the hulls on. There should be a place not too far away for storing and drying sails and somewhere for washing and changing. A night watchman may be needed too. Beach parties should be available to launch the boats if conditions are difficult. Loud-hailers are useful for catching the attention of competitors as well. Finally there can be no overhead wires between the dinghy park and the place where the boats are to be launched.

The competitors will want their sailing instructions at least forty-eight hours before the start of the first race. These instructions give the list of entrants, with their boats, sail numbers and clubs, the starting signals, times of start, the

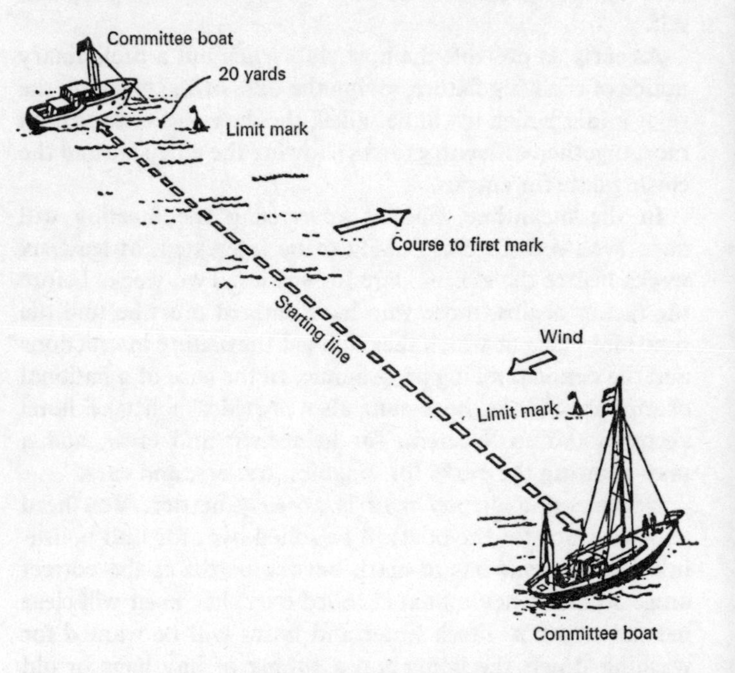

FIG. 3. A normal starting line with the wind at right-angles to the line.

sketch plans of the courses, the courses and their length, the starting and finishing lines, the method by which the course will be shortened, or the race postponed, cancelled or abandoned, the time-limit for the race, time-limit for the signing of declarations, arrangements about protests, and the names of the race officers. The sailing instructions should also say how the direction of the start will be signalled and how competitors will be told whether marks are to be left to port or to starboard. Any change in the sailing instructions must normally be notified to each competitor in writing or by signal at least fifteen minutes before the starting signal. In setting the course the Race Committee must take into account not only the weather and state of the tide but also other races likely to be in progress. The course cannot be altered later than five minutes before the start. Meantime the course has to be laid out with the necessary marks accurately placed and securely anchored. This can be quite a tricky piece of coastal navigation.The marks have to be large and conspicuous and the mark ahead must be clearly visible with the naked eye from the one behind. Ideally the position of the marks can be shown by smoke signals or even balloons sent up from a near-by committee boat. If mooring ropes are used they must be weighted in order not to get in the competitor's way.

The first leg of the course is laid more or less directly to windward to give the better boats a chance to get clear without being blanketed by the boats astern as they would be if the start were a run. Therefore the lines may have to be moved shortly before the start if the wind changes.

The starting line, laid more or less at right-angles to the wind, has to be as long as the length of the competing boats plus 25 per cent, and, in order to clear the water at either end, must have a limit mark placed on the course side of the line. Fig. 3.

It's a wonder the race ever starts. But that's not all that has to be done.

A system has to be devised for seeing that all boats get back safely from the race. Rescue launches, each with a definite patrol zone and a distinctive flag with which to call for further assistance if needed, must be ready. And of course the committee boat from which the races are started on the open sea must be powerful, easily handled, and able to fly at least three signal flags at a time from the yardarm.

The main signals are to indicate the class to which the signal applies, the warning or ten-minute signal, the preparatory or five-minutes signal before the start, the postponement, cancellation or abandonment of the race, or the shortening of course.

For this purpose the code flags of the International Code are used, as well as sound signals.

It is important to learn the International Code flags by heart, and especially the flag of the class in which you are sailing.

Ten minutes before the start of the race the flag of the class concerned is broken out and a sound signal, usually a gun, is given.

Five minutes before the start, the Blue Peter ('P' flag of the International Code) is broken and a further sound signal given and the officer of the day should start to take note of any infringements including cases of yachts that were still on their moorings at the five-minute gun. At the start, both the class flag and the Blue Peter are hauled down and a sound signal given.

In theory the gun is fired only in order to draw attention to the flag and therefore the start can be made as soon as the flag is hauled down, which is often before the sound of the gun actually reaches the ear.

The method of recalling premature starters varies and is

laid down in the sailing instructions. Some clubs fire two guns instead of one at the start to indicate that some boats are over the line and do not completely lower the class flag and Blue Peter until all yachts are clear or until a reasonable time has elapsed. They also display the recall number or numbers of the yachts concerned. Others, however, consider it impracticable to display the numbers of premature starters in the time available; they place the full responsibility for returning on the helmsman. If a large number of premature starters are over the line, the officer of the day representing the sailing committee can sound a general recall, (indicated by two more sound signals) and the first substitute flag of the International Code in preparation for a new warning signal. But this tends to encourage the bad starters (who are not disqualified) at the expense of the good, for when there is a general recall competitors are not disqualified for infringements committed before the five-minute gun for the new start. The officer of the day can also do so if there has been a mistake in timing over the start or for any other good reason. Postponement, Cancellation, Shortening Course, or Abandonment signals apply to the whole racing programme unless they are hoisted with a class flag in which case they apply to that class only. All this may sound rather academic just now but it is worth storing in the memory because there may be no one handy to explain it once you are afloat.

Postponements are reckoned from the advertised starting time of the race and *not* from the time at which the sailing committee make the postponement signal. The signal for postponing a race for fifteen minutes is the Answering Pendant of the International Code. This postponement can be extended indefinitely in fifteen-minute intervals by dipping and rehoisting the Answering Pendant. When the race is to be postponed for thirty minutes the Answering Pendant is hoisted over one ball or shape. This postponement can be extended indefinitely by adding one ball or shape for every fifteen minutes. When a race is to be postponed to a later date, the Answering Pendant is hoisted over the letter 'A' of the International Code. A gun or other sound signal must be used to call attention to the postponement signal but if you do not know your flags you may find yourself starting a race half an hour ahead of everyone else.

If the race is to be abandoned the letter 'N' of the International Code is hoisted over the class flag or race signal. If the abandonment is before the start, three guns shall be fired, but if a race is to be abandoned while still in progress the letter 'N' is shown and two guns are fired or some other sound signal made twice. If a race is to be cancelled (i.e. not resailed on another date) the flag 'X' is used.

The sailing committee may shorten the course because of wind, weather, tide or for any other good reason either before the start of a race or during it. The 'Shorten-Course' signal consists of the letter 'S' of the International Code and two guns fired. If the 'Shorten-Course' signal is to affect the whole programme, no class signals are necessary but, if it is to apply to certain races only, then the class signals of those races are shown below 'Shorten-Course' signal.

Hoisting the 'Shorten-Course' signal during the race indicates that it will finish with the round about to be completed by the leading yacht, or in any other way laid down by the sailing instructions. The officer of the day (who represents the Sailing or Race Committee) is responsible for conducting the race and for the starting and finishing arrangements, much of the fun of sailing depends on the efficiency of the officer of the day. At least three competent people are needed on the starting platform or committee boat to start a race of any size, and to check the times of the returning boats at the finish. Five people are better.

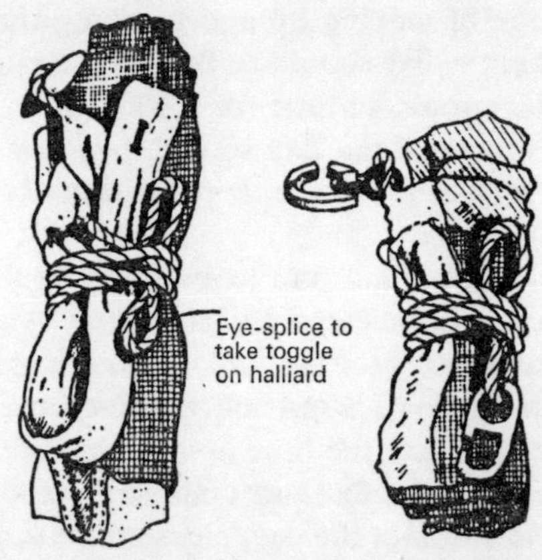

FIG. 4. Make-up of flags ready to break out.

Their equipment should include the chronometer, binoculars, guns, and ammunition (blank, smokeless) and plenty of stationery for recording purposes in addition to the flags, recall numbers, and a copy of the sailing instructions. A megaphone may be useful if there is no loud-hailer and a whistle is sometimes used for recording the finish of those boats that are not near enough to the front of the fleet to deserve a gun. A list should be made before the race of starters so that they can be accounted for afterwards.

At the start a good arrangement is to have one man call the time in seconds before the gun, a second man to warn the officer of the day about premature starters, and to note those that are actually over at the starting gun. An extra man may be needed for this purpose if recall numbers are being used or if the five-minute starting rule is in force (see Chapter 8). In theory the officer of the day should take personal responsibility for decisions as to whether a boat is across the starting line early and on the order of finishing, but if the race is a big one this is almost impossible. A fourth man should be in charge of the gun and a fifth and possibly sixth in charge of making up and breaking the flags. (It is important that the flag should be broken out and not merely hoisted at the appointed time for it.) Fig. 3.

Only the officer of the day should give any non-routine instructions such as for shortening course or abandoning the race.

At the finish it is important to get not only the order but, in handicap races, the exact finishing time. A good way of recording the finish is for the lookout to tell the timekeeper when a boat or boats approach the line, after which the timekeeper announces the time in minutes and seconds and the beginning of each subsequent minute. A second observer, preferably the officer of the day, picks up the sail numbers as they close on the line and announces 'Number so and so coming up' when the yacht has about two seconds to go. As the foremost part of the boat reaches the line he shouts 'Gun' if a gun is to be fired or 'Now' if some other signal or none at all is being given (as for example when the boat has started prematurely or is crossing the finishing line but not on the final lap). At this moment a gun is fired if required. The recorder who will already previously have noted the yacht's number when it was announced adds the time given by the timekeeper. A separate observer should check the order in which the yachts finish and a third man should make a scparate note of the finishing times called out.

But even with all this trouble the race committee may get into difficulties, as I found one afternoon when seven yachts finished within five seconds of each other in a direction that made it almost impossible to pick out the sail numbers.

During a big championship, the competitors will want to know their positions as soon as possible after the end of the race, so will the newspapers. So it's a good idea to have a special score team and well-designed score-sheets for such emergencies.

3. A Flying Dutchman planing on a broad reach. This photo was taken at Whitstable during a European Championship in this exciting, racing class. Note the crew out on the trapeze.

4. Fireflies at Gorleston in squally weather. The nearer dinghy looks down by the head, possibly because she has shipped water. The race was later abandoned when the wind strengthened and most of the fleet retired or capsized.

Sometimes in small clubs it isn't easy to find people willing to serve on the Race Committee, since the people who know most about the game are the ones that want to race themselves. However one solution is for the Sailing Committee to put up a notice on the club board listing race officers for each racing fixture. Those named are responsible for finding substitutes if they cannot themselves attend.

Believe me the only way to understand the difficulties of organizing a race is to give up sailing for a season and do it yourself.

4

The Spirit of the Rules

When a sailing vessel is afloat (or even aground) but not racing, she is subject to the International Regulations for Preventing Collisions at Sea (IRPCAS) in force since September 1965 and obtainable through any nautical or Government bookshop.

The various day and night signals (lights, displayed shapes, bells, whistles, etc.) of IRPCAS are a study in themselves and far too detailed to summarize here.

But on the question of right of way the main points to remember are:

1. A sailing boat has right of way over a power boat except in narrow channels where the power-driven vessel cannot manœuvre. Also, the sailing boat may not 'hamper' the power boat and if collision cannot be avoided by the action of the power boat alone the sailing boat must take avoiding action.
2. As between sailing boats that are not racing:
   (*a*) *On opposite tacks* the vessel which has the wind on the port side shall keep out of the way of the other.
   (*b*) *On the same tack* the boat to windward shall keep out the way of the vessel to leeward.
   (*c*) *On either tack* an overtaking boat must keep clear.

The IRPCAS rules say that you should not cross close ahead of a right of way vessel.

Both (*a*) and (*b*) apply to vessels both when racing and when not racing but there is an important difference between the racing rules and the non-racing rules governing overtaking boats.

When both boats are racing if the overtaking boat has the wind on her starboard side and the leading boat is carrying her mainsail on the opposite side (i.e. is on port tack) then the latter even though in the lead must keep clear. When a racing yacht meets another non-racing vessel the IRPCAS rules apply, and the overtaking boat must keep clear even when she is on starboard tack.

Yachts that are not racing sometimes give way to those that are racing even when the latter have no right of way. But this is only a matter of courtesy.

Racing yachts of course are distinguishable from others because of the rectangular racing flag which they fly in British waters.

Having I hope eliminated the non-racers, let us have a look at the rules in force between the rest of us.

They made the rules of yacht racing with two objects in view:

Firstly to encourage fair sailing (therefore the helmsman, in his own interests as well as those of others, should learn just what rights he has or has not in any given situation), and secondly to avoid unnecessary risk; and, since most exciting racing takes place at close quarters, if not within collision distance, knowledge of rules helps to avoid expensive insurance claims as well as lost races and long absences while the boat is ashore for repairs.

When do the racing rules apply?

Some of them particularly the Sailing Rules when yachts meet apply 'between yachts which either are intending to race or are racing in the same or different races . . . from the time a yacht intending to race begins to sail about in the vicinity of the starting line until she has either finished or retired and has left the vicinity of the Starting Line'.

Therefore from the time a boat arrives near the starting line intending to race she must behave like a racing boat towards other boats racing or intending to race.

But at the same time a yacht cannot be *disqualified* for infringing a Right of Way racing rule unless the infringement occurs while she is racing (i.e. after the five-minute gun) whether or not a collision results.

Now this chapter and the next do not pretend to cover every clause of yacht racing's seventy-eight rules. But at least everything here is based on the newly introduced code (1965) and there is enough to save anyone who is starting to race from doing so in blinkers, as it were.

Britain, like every other country belonging to the International Yacht Racing Union, races under rules known as the 1965–68 rules. Up till 1961 there had been wide differences between the IYRU Rules and those used by the North American Yacht Racing Union since 1946. Today these differences have almost completely disappeared.

In the United Kingdom the IYRU Rule is interpreted by the Royal Yachting Association.

These rules obtainable from the RYA are not difficult to understand and the most important of them runs as follows:

> Rule 49—Fair Sailing. A yacht shall attempt to win a race only by fair sailing, superior speed and skill and except in team races, by individual effort.

Those words are the essence of the whole affair.

The term 'fair sailing' is a wide one. The rule applies before and after racing as well as during. It obviously excludes illegal means of propulsion such as waggling the tiller or artificially flapping the mainsail but an oar or paddle may be used for steering in an emergency.

Yacht racing, perhaps because of the absence of a 'gallery' or a 'gate' has remained an amateur sport. Every yacht during a race must have on board an amateur who belongs to a yacht or sailing club recognized by a national authority, and who is in charge of the yacht as the owner or owner's representative. (An amateur is a yachtsman who engages in yachting activities afloat as a pastime as distinct from a means of obtaining a livelihood. He must not accept any profitable benefit as remuneration or inducement for participation in yacht racing.)

In International races, anyone going overboard during a race whether accidentally or otherwise must, unless injured or ill, or unless assisting someone in peril, be taken aboard again before the yacht continues the race. But in United Kingdom races, the RYA places no restrictions on anyone going ashore from a yacht during a race provided that neither class rules nor sailing instructions forbid it.

All yachts are expected to give help to people or boats in trouble. If any yacht not responsible in the judgement of the sailing committee for a misfortune to another vessel injures her chances of winning any prize through giving assistance, the sailing committee may order the race to be re-sailed. A yacht neglecting to give help when in a position to do so to any person or boat in peril may be disqualified. This disqualification is not however automatic since if other boats are nearer to the victim or a launch is already within sight, there may be no need for every boat in a position to give help to do so.

Under British Rules a racing boat must fly a rectangular distinguishing flag (of which the hoist and fly shall be not less than one third of the size of the numbers on her mainsail), which must not be hauled down unless she gives up the race. She must carry numbers showing her class and sail number and if necessary her nationality, on both sides of the mainsail at about two-thirds of the height of the sail so that they are still visible when the sail is fully reefed. The sail numbers should be sewn on the sail at different heights on the two sides to avoid confusion through the transparency of the sail. The spinnaker need carry only the sail numbers on each side, and not letters as well.

After a race, the man in charge of the yacht during the race will be required to sign a declaration confirming that all rules and sailing instructions were obeyed during the race. The sailing instructions usually lay down the time-limit within which the declaration must be lodged or posted.

When on the water it is important to remember the right-of-way rules which are designed to avoid collisions and not to press them too far. Thus a yacht may not tack into a right-of-way position so as to involve the probability of collision with another yacht which owing to her position cannot keep out of the way. And she, as well as the other yacht, can be disqualified if she makes no attempt to avoid a collision resulting in serious damage, except when she is luffing a boat to windward. In all other situations she must hail before or when making an alteration of course which may not be foreseen by the other yacht or when claiming room at a mark or obstruction. She must hail when she is aground or out of control to give warning that she has become an obstruction to sea room.

Anchoring after the five-minute gun is allowed and may be carried out by the crew standing on the bottom, but a boat may not be made fast by other means than these. She may be hauled out solely in order to reef, bale out, refloat after grounding or carry out repairs, provided she is not assisted by persons not members of her crew unless they belong to a vessel with which she has collided. Every effort must be made to recover an anchor used in a race before continuing.

Now since the right-of-way yacht must normally avoid collisions, except in certain circumstances when luffing a boat to windward, it follows that the other yacht which obstructs her may be disqualified whether or not a collision takes place. Thus if a right-of-way starboard yacht has to bear away or luff up to avoid hitting a port-tack boat, the latter has broken the rules just as surely as if a collision had taken place.

A helmsman need not feel guilty about hoisting a protest flag if he has genuinely had to make a detour when he had the right of way. In fact the standard of sailing at a club can fall rapidly if too few protests are made. It is unfair to continue to stay in a race after having broken a rule if you are certain that you are at fault. The rule on this is definite. This makes it clear that having broken a rule a yacht must retire at once and haul down her racing flag to show that she is doing so; it is not permissible for her to continue racing and to salve her conscience later by not signing the declaration.

Most breaches of the rules occur when a helmsman takes a chance that does not quite come off, or because he fails to foresee the situation which is about to arise. Certainly these sins are to be avoided as they may spoil the race for other boats apart from causing damage through a collision.

But the helmsman who is at fault can at least expiate his crime by retiring. If he sails on after having broken a rule through his own fault, he is not only evading the penalty but is also being unfair to his competitors; and he is setting a bad example to other helmsmen which, in the long run, will be against his own interests as well for, in practice, it is seldom possible for the Sailing Committee to arrange for a resail although they are entitled to do so.

Retiring right away will lose him the race and perhaps some good sailing but at any rate will not lose him his friends.

5

The Rules in Action

The most exciting moments in racing occur when boats are at close quarters and in such crises it is vital to know exactly what course you are entitled to take in the presence of another boat.

Two rules are generally recognized as fundamental. *First: That when two yachts meet on opposite tacks (or gybes) the one having the wind on her starboard side has the right of way.*

There are only two exceptions to this port and starboard rule when racing. The first occurs when a yacht has made a premature start and is working her way back on starboard tack to the right side of the line to make a new start, in which case she has no rights at all until she is behind the line. (But the other yachts shall not assume that a yacht is returning or working into position from the wrong side of the line until her manœuvres are obviously inconsistent with an intention to continue sailing the course.)

The other exception occurs when two boats on opposite tacks with the wind aft are overlapping and about to pass on the required side of a mark of the course or on the same side of an obstruction to sea room, in which case the outside yacht (even if she is on starboard tack and would otherwise hold the right of way) must give room to the inside yacht to pass or round the mark or obstruction.

The Second fundamental rule refers to yachts on the same

tack. In this case the windward yacht must keep clear of the leeward.

Neither of these fundamental rules gives any boat right of way over another merely on the ground that she is close hauled and the other not, though this was formerly the case.

Suppose now, under this second windward-leeward fundamental rule, we take the case of one boat which is trying to pass another to leeward. At what point does the windward overtaken boat have to keep clear and how does she do so?

In the first place unless the boats are on a windward course the leading boat must not sail below (to leeward of) her proper course (the one she would have sailed if the other boat had not been present) when she is clearly within *three of her over-all lengths* of a leeward yacht or of a yacht clear astern which is steering a course to pass to leeward (if the boats are on a windward course, i.e. the boats must tack on their course for the next mark, then bearing away is permitted though the windward boat must still keep clear).

A yacht is *clear astern* of another when her hull, spars, and sails are aft of an imaginary line drawn abeam from the

FIG. 5.

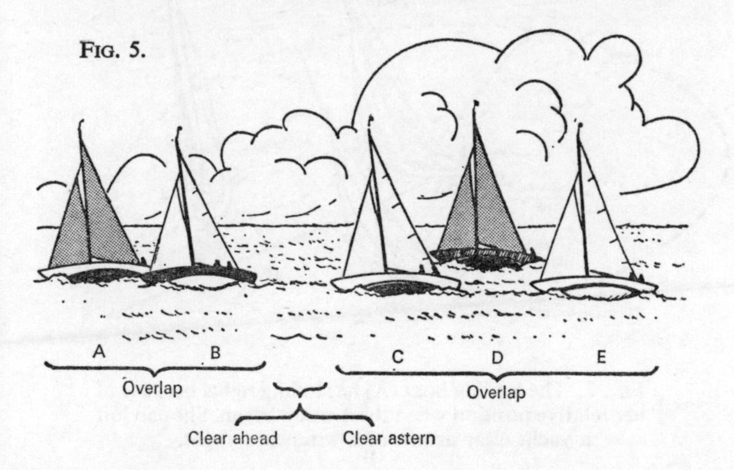

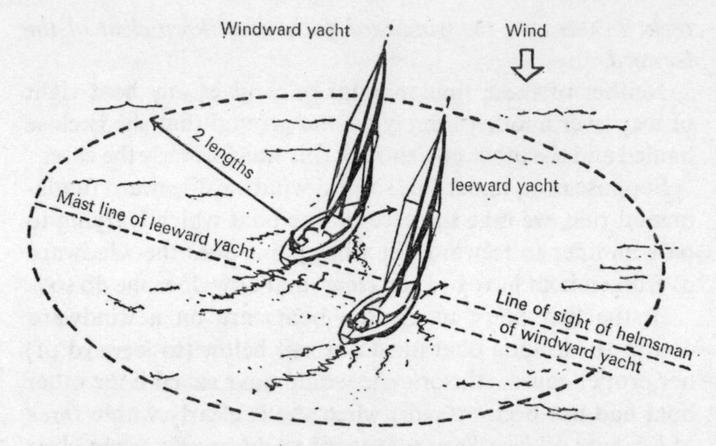

FIG. 6. This overlap began without luffing rights for the leeward yacht, who must now not sail above her proper course while the overlap exists.

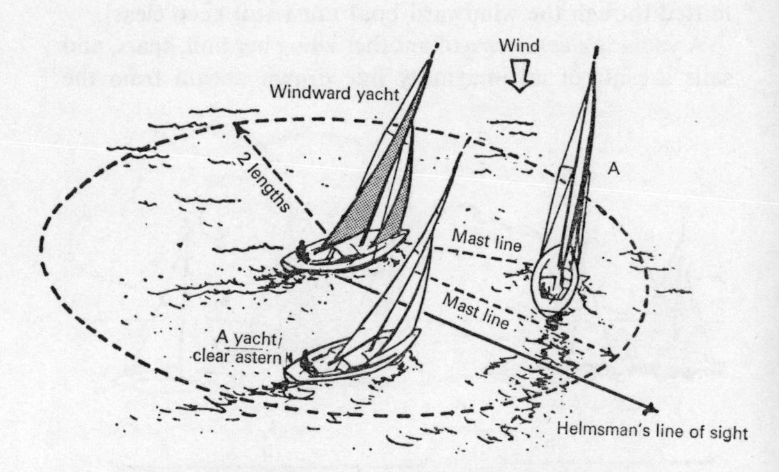

FIG. 7. The leading boat (A) has luffing rights because of her relative position when the overlap began. She can luff a yacht clear astern or a windward yacht.

aftermost part of the other's hull and spars. The other yacht is then clear ahead. If the overtaking yacht continues to gain she eventually ceases to be clear astern. In this case, if neither yacht is clear ahead but the yachts are clearly within *two over-all lengths* of the longer yacht, an overlap is said to exist between them. Fig. 5.

If, when the overlap began, the helmsman of the windward yacht when sighting abeam from his normal station was forward of the mainmast of the leeward yacht, the latter may not sail above her proper course while that overlap continues to exist, and cannot luff the windward yacht. Fig. 6. But if the leeward yacht approaches from close astern and on the proper course the windward yacht must keep clear.

Otherwise a yacht that has crossed and cleared the starting line may luff a yacht clear astern or a windward yacht as suddenly as she pleases and head to wind if she likes to prevent her passing even at the risk of collision, until the point where the helmsman of the windward yacht when sighting abeam from his normal station *and sailing no higher than the leeward yacht* comes abreast of the mainmast of the leeward yacht. Fig. 7.

In case of doubt the leeward yacht may assume that she has the right to luff unless the helmsman of the windward yacht has hailed 'Mast Abeam' or words to that effect.

The leeward yacht must respect that hail and if she thinks it improper her only remedy is to protest. Once having reached the mast abeam position she must bear away and must not again sail above her proper course whilst the same overlap exists.

The windward yacht must not cause the luff to be cut short through not keeping clear of the leeward yacht, unless an obstruction is in the way and she had got an overlap on the leeward yacht before reaching it. A yacht must not luff unless she has the right to luff all yachts which would be affected by her luff, in which case they must all respond, even if an intervening yacht or yachts would not otherwise have the right to luff. Except when she is allowed to luff, a right-of-way yacht may not alter her course so as to prevent another yacht from keeping out of her way and she must not alter course in such a way as to mislead or baulk the other in the act of keeping out of the way. But a yacht is not misleading or baulking another if she alters course by luffing or bearing away to conform to a change in the strength or direction of the wind.

It has now just been decided that a starboard tack yacht is not allowed to luff above a close-hauled course in order to prevent a port tack yacht from crossing ahead and so this counts as 'misleading'.

A yacht which is tacking or gybing must keep clear of a yacht which is not doing so and if two yachts are tacking or gybing at the same time, the one on the other's port side shall keep clear.

When a yacht tacks or gybes into a position which will subsequently give her right-of-way, she must do so far enough away from a yacht so that the latter need not begin to keep clear until the tack or gybe is completed and then still have room to keep clear. A yacht may not tack so as to risk probable collision with another yacht which, owing to her position, cannot keep out of the way. This could well be the case where one starboard tack yacht threatens a whole row of port tack yachts who cannot go about simultaneously.

Coming now to marks and obstructions the rule is that if after the start of the race, two yachts overlap on the same tack when one of them is about to round or pass a mark on the required side, or an obstruction to sea room which they are to pass on the same side, the outside yacht must give the inside yacht room to pass or round.

This also applies to yachts on opposite tacks except when close-hauled or where one of the yachts will have to tack to round the mark or avoid the obstruction. The overlap must however have been made before the leading boat came within two of her own lengths from the mark or obstruction. If not, the yacht clear astern shall keep clear in anticipation of and during the rounding or passing manœuvre.

Room to round the mark includes room to tack or gybe if this is a part of the rounding manœuvre of the two boats but this does not give the leading yacht freedom to tack just ahead of another yacht which is sailing close-hauled. In each case you should hail the other boat as soon as an overlap has been madc to give warning that water will be required.

If a close-hauled yacht has to make a substantial alteration of course to avoid an obstruction, and cannot tack without colliding with a close-hauled yacht on the same tack, she may hail the latter for room to tack.

The yacht that has been hailed must either tack at the earliest possible moment after the hail, in which case the yacht that has called for water must tack at once, beginning if possible before the hailed yacht has completed her tack; or she must reply 'You tack' or words to that effect if in her opinion she can keep clear of the other yacht without tacking or after postponing her tack. In this case the yacht that has called for water shall immediately tack and the hailed yacht shall keep clear. The onus of satisfying the race committee that she kept clear lies with the hailed yacht.

In such cases the windward yacht often has to give up considerable advantage and therefore the rule takes care to make one important exception. If the obstruction in question is a mark of the course which the windward yacht can fetch, the leeward yacht shall not be entitled to room to tack and the hailed yacht shall at once inform her of this. If after this warning the hailing yacht again calls for water she shall be given room to tack but must after receiving it retire at once. If the yacht that was hailed refuses to give room but fails to fetch the mark she must retire at once.

If a leeward yacht decides to clear an obstruction by bearing away she must allow the yacht to windward to do the same if she wants to. If a yacht fouls a mark while rounding or passing it, including a starting mark before the start or a finishing mark after the finish (for you are still 'racing' until you have crossed *and cleared* the finishing line and finishing marks) she must retire at once from the race unless she was compelled to foul it by another yacht, in which case she must protest.

The rule about giving room at marks also provides for the special circumstances prevailing at the start of the race. Then, only too often, there is a temptation for yachts to

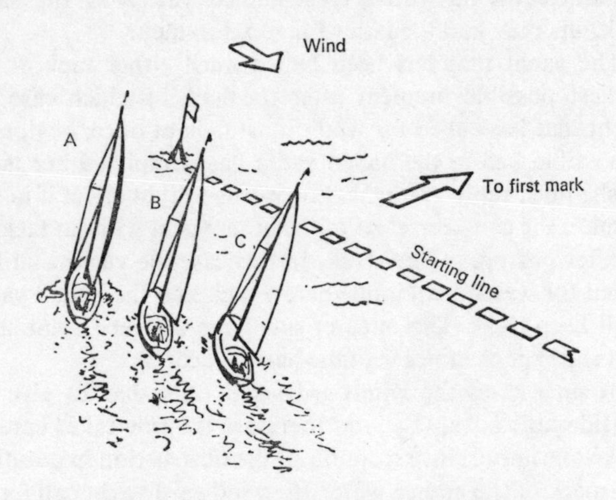

FIG. 8. Barging at the start (1) – the situation before the starting signal. Boat B cannot call for water before the start in spite of her overlap.

barge in at the windward end of the line causing dangerous congestion there. So a regulation has been framed—if that is the right word—to protect yachts starting on a proper course for the first mark.

This regulation says that when coming up to the starting line to start, a leeward yacht is under no obligation to give room to any windward yacht on the same tack to pass to leeward of a mark of the starting line that is surrounded by navigable water. Now this situation applies up to the very last instant before the starting signal is made. Fig. 8. It follows therefore that whatever the course for the first mark, a boat that is to windward of a close-hauled course for the limit mark of the starting line can be frozen out the wrong side of the mark by a boat which is approaching the starting line on her final run in to start.

Once the starting signal has been made, however, a lee-

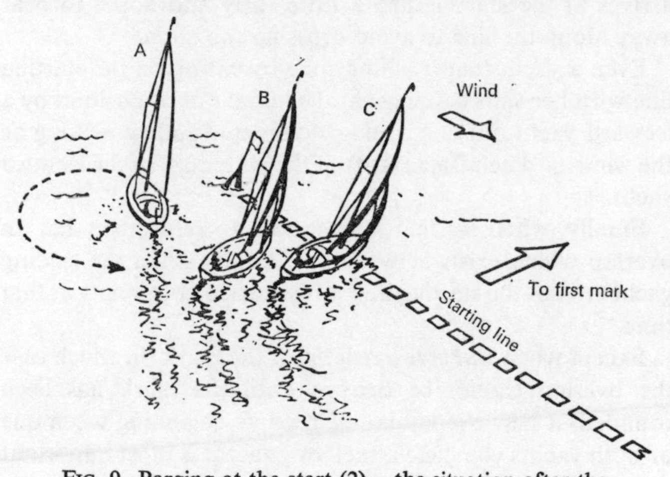

FIG. 9. Barging at the start (2) – the situation after the signal with a reaching start. Boat C must not sail above her proper course for the first mark if this obstructs B at the mark.

ward right-of-way yacht shall not deprive a windward yacht of room at the mark by sailing above her proper course for the first mark in the course if the wind be free or by luffing above a close-hauled course if on the wind. Fig. 9.

Before the start there is no proper course since the yacht in question may be merely killing time or sailing away from the line and her movements cannot always be foreseen or anticipated. Therefore before the starting line has been crossed and cleared, if a yacht clear ahead or to leeward wants to alter her course in such a way as to affect another yacht she must do so only slowly and a leeward yacht may luff only when the helmsman of the windward yacht is aft of the mainmast of the leeward yacht. But even though there is no proper course before the start a windward yacht may not bear away so as to force any leeward yacht to alter course. This particular rule is often a great nuisance if one arrives at the starting line a little early and hopes to bear away along the line to avoid crossing too soon.

Even a yacht that is killing time by sitting on the starting line with her sails flapping can be luffed out of position by a leeward yacht altering course slowly and luffing as long as the windward helmsman is aft of the mainmast of the leeward yacht.

Finally, when starting it is as well to remember that an overlap which exists between two yachts when the leading yacht crosses the starting line is regarded as beginning at that time.

Except when *within two lengths* of the mark (in which case the overlap cannot be broken until the mark has been rounded) a new overlap is regarded as beginning when one or both yachts complete a tack or gybe. It is most important to remember this since your position at the time when you and the other boat change from 'other tack' to 'same tack' positions will decide whether you have luffing rights over

5. Ospreys rounding a mark at Hayling Island during a championship week. Possibly the tide has prevented them from rounding closely.

6. Over 100 National 12 dinghies cross the line at Scarborough at the start of a Burton Week race. This is when it pays to have a gate start.

that yacht or not. The overlap is broken when one yacht widens out beyond three over-all lengths of the longer yacht or draws clear ahead or astern.

And if you are like me you will always heave a sigh of relief when this happens especially if yours is the yacht that has drawn clear ahead.

You may not use a paddle until after the finishing line has been cleared in order to avoid hitting a finishing mark since the rule forbidding abnormal means of propulsion applies until a yacht has finished racing that is until she has cleared the finishing line *and finishing marks.*

It would be impossible in a book of this length to go in detail into the rules of yacht racing. But for those interested I would strongly recommend *Paul Elvstrom Explains** published in Britain by Richard Creagh-Osborne and partners. This pocket-size book takes the rules one by one and interprets them with diagrams. The book also contains in its cover a plastic set of four model boats, with indicators for buoys and wind-direction which can be used for representing all manner of situations affected by the rules. There are well over one hundred valuable eye-openers and I should strongly recommend all who enjoy racing to invest in this little work.

* Distributed by Adlard Coles Ltd, 3 Upper James St., Golden Square, London W1.

6

Crewing

There are two entirely different kinds of crewing; in large boats and small. Each has its attractions for the newcomer.

In a large and splendid boat the duties are often uncomplicated and neatly shared out so that one is apt to find oneself in charge of a single object such as a winch. Then, after perhaps a season's racing round the buoys one can qualify as a specialist say on the spinnaker or, in ocean racing, as a cook or bosun or radio expert. Life therefore *can* be relatively simple.

But in a small boat you are the whole front part of the ship from the word 'go' and will probably be dealing from the start not only with the jib and spinnaker, if any, but also with the centre-plate and, in some boats, with the trapeze as well.

As there are many more small boats than large, the newcomer will probably start small and thereby quickly learn a little about everything.

So far we have talked about crews as if they were all masculine. But that is a piece of over-simplification. Many small boats are designed to be sailed with a helmsman and crew weighing about twenty stone combined, i.e. for mixed sailing. Some small boat owners are women who prefer men crews for their weight (if for no other reason). But even more boat owners are men who rely enthusiastically on women for crewing. These women crews are often quite beyond praise. Perhaps they find it natural to aid and comfort the helmsman and to feed his vanity. (With a woman you seldom if ever have the feeling that she would like to be steering the boat herself). In other cases a woman crew excels because she likes to know that her boat can always be among the leaders and that she can crew as well as any man, which she usually can if the boat is not too big.

So if I merely say 'he' when writing of helmsmen or crews it is only to simplify the wording and no discrimination is intended.

The ideal crew has a fighting spirit of the kind that helps him to aid recovery from the worst possible start. Other qualities especially valuable in a small boat are quick reactions, good strength for his weight, a sense of balance, willingness to learn, punctuality and unquestioning obedience.

A crew will find that every yacht has her own distinct personality; for, even in a one-design boat, the fittings and lay-out vary. Sometimes a crew may find that the cleats or fairleads are unsuitably placed, in which case he should not be afraid to suggest improvements. The helmsman will probably be only too glad to know about these.

Some helmsmen are the strong silent kind who wrestle with themselves and say almost nothing. Others give tongue almost continuously—though incoherently. A few shout at the crew—and don't mean all that they say. But perhaps they are preferable to the over-polite skippers who pass an order as though they were asking for permission to open a railway carriage window. Aggression is a quality which crews look for and appreciate in their skipper.

A lot depends on the relative experience of the helmsman and crew. They should be of about the same standard. If the crew is inferior to the helmsman he will not understand the tactics (and there will be no time to explain them). If on the other hand the crew is more advanced he will wish he had steered the boat himself (yes! even if they win).

Practice of course is essential. Yet how many times in a season do we see a boat out practising gybes round a mark or even timing starts? Most crews hope to learn some racing technique from their skippers and practice sailing gives the best opportunity for this. It is also good training for the crew to take the helm from time to time either in a crew's race or on the way home after finishing the course.

The division of the duties between helmsman and crew varies considerably from boat to boat. Sometimes, in a husband and wife combination, the husband crews on the beat when strenuous sitting out is required while the wife crews on the run when a light foot is required on the fore-deck. In other cases the crew acts as navigator or tactician while the helmsman concentrates on making the boat go on the course set.

Some helmsmen like to be told of every approaching boat and of every windshift. Others can see these things for themselves or pretend they can and prefer not to be distracted. If you have long sight and have spotted the next mark, the helmsman will almost certainly be glad to know. But don't point unless you want to pass the news to a rival helmsman. The same applies to signals made by the sailing committee. On the other hand it is only too easy for the crew to become a back-seat driver, so to speak, by commenting on how well the other boats are doing. I find that is almost worse than a 'couldn't-care-less' attitude.

When crewing, every little counts. A variation of an inch or two in the crew's position will noticeably alter the trim of a small boat and may make the difference between planing and not planing. The same applies to the job of playing the jib in and out correctly during a reach.

So if the skipper of a small boat says 'Jib in a little' or 'Plate up slightly' you can usually take the order literally.

In the past few years there has been an increase in the

duties required of small boat crews. One popular type of racing boat, the Hornet, is fitted with a sliding plank on which the crew sits outside the boat with his feet on the gunwale when extra weight is necessary to keep the boat level.

In boats such as the Five-O-Five, Flying Dutchman and Tempest, crews have had to learn how to stand on the gunwale, being supported at the waist by a belt clipped to a trapeze wire rigged to the mast.

Naturally there is a shortage of well-trained crews who are content not to be helmsmen. Some clubs however have had success with a crew list assembled by circularizing a suitably worded application form which, when completed, shows the crews' address, telephone number, age, experience, availability, and inclinations. For small boat work it is also worth knowing the weight of the crew.

By the way there is not an official trade union for crews although those in the sharp end of the boat often feel that there ought to be.

But once the race is over you qualify for a long, long, or long, short drink.

7

Preparing for the Start

The night before is not too soon to begin getting ready for the starting signal. For one thing there is the weather forecast, which in turn affects the clothes and equipment needed as well as the time taken to get to the club by road. For a heavy day, waterproof buoyancy jackets and perhaps reefing gear may be needed as well as flat sails and thick sail battens.

For a light day the kedge may be essential if the wind drops and a paddle too in case you decide to give up for lack of wind.

The tide can be studied the night before the race, and, when on the water, some helmsmen work from carefully prepared hour to hour tide charts. The higher the tide the stronger the current will run, and if the starting line is some distance up current from the mooring, extra time may be needed to get there during spring tides. Often the shape of a channel and its peculiarities change between high water and low.

The sailing instructions and even the advertisement of the race always contain information that it is profitable to study, especially when the race is being sailed at an unfamiliar club.

It is also very useful to be able to form a picture in your mind of the starting line, of the various courses and of the finishing line. Often there is one finishing line if the complete course is sailed and another if the course has to be shortened. Some people make out charts showing the compass bearing from one mark to the next and use a compass when sailing on open waters.

The routine of the day of the race largely depends on whether the boat is kept afloat or on moorings.

The sails are usually kept at home or in the sail room at the club. In either case the crew should make an early check in order to bc able to fetch them if they have been left at home or to find them if they have strayed from their usual place in the sail drying-room. Sometimes the battens are kept aboard the boat; sometimes not. Get to know which.

The same applies to movable property such as the tiller, the spinnaker boom, the racing flag, the bailer or hand-pump, and the like. Calamity could follow any of these items being left ashore. Then there is the stop-watch. Many people buy a special instrument for timing at the start but there is little need for this if your watch has a big second hand and is waterproof. I have had and used my £10 watch for many sailing seasons (as well as during the rest of the year), and, apart from having it regularly cleaned, the only precaution I take is to smear a little thick grease round the edge of the face and the winding stem each spring.

So-called waterproof watches vary considerably in efficiency. Most will withstand a wetting from spray, but the big test comes with a capsize on a really hot day. Then, as the watch dips into the water, its temperature falls sharply and the air inside the case contracts and this steps up the external pressure very rapidly, by setting up a partial vacuum.

Sometimes a watch that has got wet inside can be saved by keeping it immersed in alcohol, petrol or other light oil until it can be cleaned by a jeweller, but the chances of recovery are greatly reduced if salt water has got into the works.

To return to the morning of the race, it may often be difficult to make really detailed plans until within an hour or two of the start. Sometimes there is a local airfield whose meteorological expert can be called to the telephone to give the latest on the weather. Otherwise one has to rely on the regional weather forecast whose predictions in your particular locality may come true earlier or later than expected or even not at all.

If the sky is clear on a hot day you are more likely to have a sea breeze setting in about midday than if there are clouds.

Some clubs have an instrument for measuring the strength and direction of the wind and this helps one to weigh up the conditions on the water. Otherwise it may not be easy to judge conditions from the shore.

For example any shore observation post is liable to be more sheltered on one side than on another, and, if the wind goes round to the protected side one is apt to conclude that it has dropped. The same applies if you look out to sea when the wind is blowing off-shore. The size of waves and white horses aren't nearly as obvious as they would be if the wind were blowing on-shore. After allowing for the strength and direction of the wind and other local weather indications it may be possible to foretell the probable conditions at the beginning, middle, and end of the race.

If the current is going to be against the wind you can expect the water to be choppy to a degree depending on the strength of the wind and the rate of the current.

You may also expect that the beat will be more strenuous because the force of the current will add to the speed of the apparent wind. On the other hand the beat will be shorter than it would have been if the wind and current had been running in the same direction.

Once the course has been announced you can work out the race tactics in greater detail, and decide at which end of

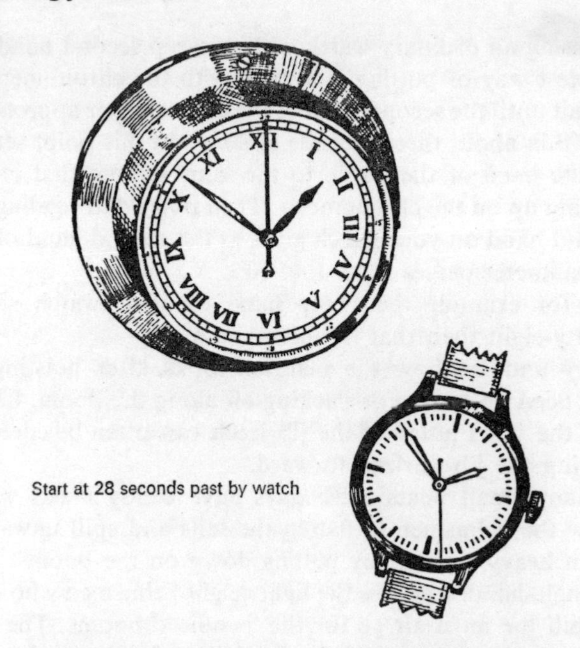

FIG. 10. To set a watch by a chronometer, adjust the watch minute hand to the same minute as the chronometer minute hand, and note the difference between the second hands when that of the chronometer next reaches the 60 mark. In the example above, you would start when the watch second hand reads 28 seconds past.

the line to start. You can also consider whether it will pay to stand in or out from the shore and whether a spinnaker will be set during the race and if so on which side. Remember that wind tends to cross the shore at right angles and that wind pouring through a gap tends to fan out in many different directions.

Finally it is easier to check the stop-watch with the chronometer before going afloat rather than on the water. If you are using an ordinary watch with a sweep second hand the simplest way of putting it in time with the chronometer is to wait until the second hand of the chronometer approaches to within about three seconds of sixty. At this point set the minute hand of the watch to the same minute that is just coming up on the chronometer. Then note what reading the second hand on your watch gives as the second hand of the chronometer passes sixty. Fig. 10.

If for example the sweep hand on your watch shows twenty-eight then that is where you start.

Try and see how the mainsail looks after hoisting. It may need tightening or slacking off along the boom. Check also the jib. Flutter of the jib leech can often be cured by moving the jib fairlead forward.

Many small boats these days have bendy masts which allow the helmsmen to flatten the sails and spill unwanted air in heavy weather by pulling down on the booms. And in single-handed classes the lightweight helmsmen who need to spill the most air go for the 'bendiest' booms. The sail-maker in turn must take the flexibility of the mast into account when designing the sail.

As for the rig, some say the boat goes better if the shrouds are loose enough to allow considerable free play to the mast. Others consider that floppy rigging leads to broken masts. There's something to be said for both these views.

The important thing is to see that the shrouds are evenly tensioned and that the mast has no sideways kinks when under strain.

Terylene sails may appear virtually indestructible but they do need *some* care. They may not stretch much but they *do* have a designed shape and should be allowed to assume it from the start. In other words don't assume that it will be okay to hoist your new sail bar taut up the mast and along the boom the first time you take it out.

Terylene sails can be put away wet even after having been soaked with sea water without mildew attacking the cloth itself. But you may get marks where the mildew fungus has attacked the dressing or dye. Furthermore salt left on the sails does rub off the wax filler which is put there both to give the sail a smooth finish and to make it 'air-proof'. Salt will also attract moisture and add to the weight of the sail.

So a freshwater wash is indicated from time to time.

When storing, fold the sails loosely with the creases as far as possible parallel to the direction in which the wind blows across them. For dinghy owners: when leaving for the race. Don't forget to put in the draining plugs. It is surprising how much water pours in before you notice.

8

The Start

What a mad, not-so-merry moment the start of a race can be!

Boats rushing at one from all quarters, the water churned up as though by a washing-machine and that second hand ticking away all the time on one's wrist. Sometimes you don't know which way to sail in order not to arrive early, but an instant's hesitation can mean a disastrous start or perhaps even disqualification. No wonder hundreds of thousands of words have been written on how to make the perfect getaway. First, make sure which end of the line is nearer to windward (It is the end your boat points nearer to when she is head to wind). Then although you may have decided which end of the line you prefer, it is still a good idea to see how long it takes to get from one end of the line to the other. You may want to get across there if the wind shifts. These two moves will give you your bearings. Check the speed of the current by watching your own track when travelling across it.

It is not enough to cross the starting line a split second after the starting gun; one must also be travelling at speed and with right of way, and at a point giving the easiest course for the next mark.

Suppose we take these essentials one by one. First the time.

The easiest way of getting to the line at the right moment is to make a trial run from some known position to the point where you intend crossing and note the time taken. If the time taken is 'x' seconds, you make your final run-up to the start beginning 'x' seconds before the starting gun is to fire. This works well enough on the whole, except that, when all the boats are starting for the line at the same time and are lee-bowing and back-winding each other, progress is likely to be slower.

If the race is being run close to the shore or in an estuary, it may be fairly easy to find the starting point for your trial run by lining up objects on the shore; or there may even be a moored boat or mooring handy.

But if the starting line is on the open sea as happens in most championships, it may be easier to work on another principle; the 'there and back' system.

For this purpose you begin your practice start at the point where you mean to cross the starting line and travel in the reverse direction so that in which you intend starting. Sail in this reverse direction say for twenty seconds, then turn

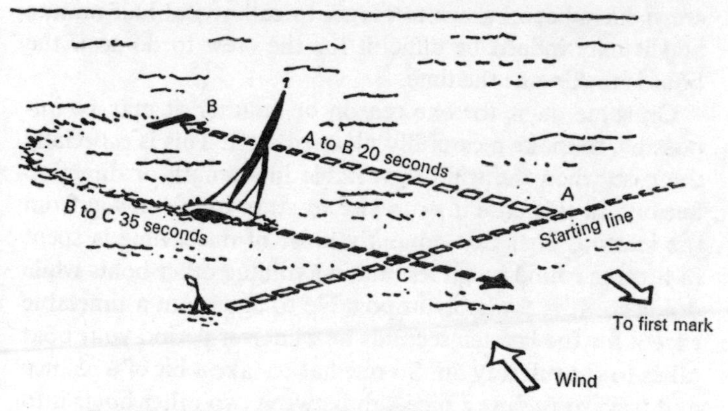

FIG. 11. A 'there-and-back' start for use in the open sea. The yacht commences her starting run from A to C at the starting gun time less 55 seconds.

and sail for the line and note the time when you recross it. Suppose the return journey takes thirty-five seconds including turning time. You then know that for your final run up you must leave the starting line with fifty-five seconds to go and commence your final turn when there are thirty-five seconds left. This is the theory of the system, but, like many other things, it may need adjustment to put it into practice. Fig. 11.

Some helmsmen prefer their crews to call out the time before the start and in this case it may be convenient to have each minute called after the ten-minute gun, each half-minute after the five-minute gun and each five seconds down to the last ten seconds which are called individually.

Other helmsmen prefer to do the timing themselves because this allows them to get the time at any instant without having to ask—even though looking at a watch may mean taking one's eye off the ball for a moment.

There is probably something to be said for both helmsman and crew keeping an eye on the time. Certainly some crews have been known to forget to call a vital half-minute and it may indeed be difficult for the crew to do so if the boat is tacking at the time.

On some days, for one reason or another, it may be impossible to make a carefully planned start. This is especially the case when the wind is variable in strength or direction because in this case it is unwise to stray too far away from the starting line. Consequently most of one's time is spent in turning round in circles and in avoiding other boats while doing so. It is probably impossible to figure out a timetable except for the last ten seconds or whatever period your boat takes to get full way on. So one has to take a bit of a chance and trust to finding a nice gap between two other boats into which one can safely plunge just before the starting signal goes. Don't take all way off the boat by frequent last minute tacks unless of course you decide to 'hover' almost on the line until a few seconds before the starting gun. On the starting line the real danger comes from boats to leeward which prevent you from bearing away and getting full way on. Avoid them wherever possible.

The odds against finding a gap vary according to the number of starters and the length of the line. Naturally when making a last-minute start it is all the more important to do so from a position which will give you the right of way—in other words on starboard tack or gybe.

This means when the course to the first mark is a beat and the course is at right-angles to the wind the ideal start has to be made from the extreme windward end of the line in order to avoid being blanketed by other boats. Consequently competition for the windward position is apt to be intense. It was for this reason that a special rule was introduced to

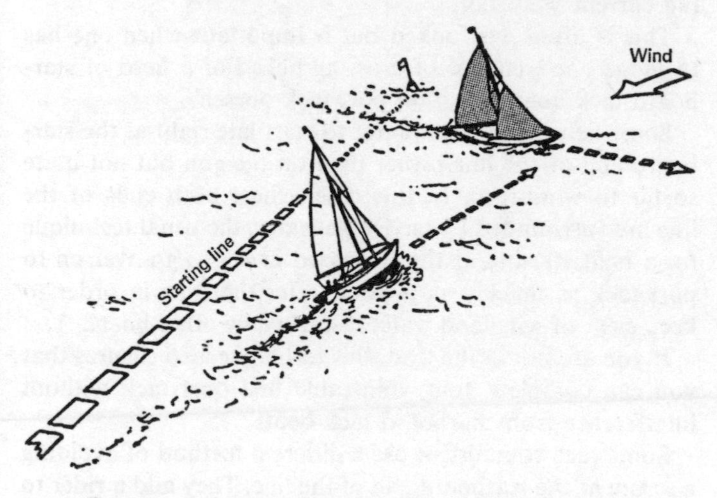

FIG. 12. A tilted starting line. This encourages a port tack start and avoids overcrowding at the starboard end of the line.

discourage boats from barging down on the starting mark from points upwind of it.

Various other ways of discouraging overcrowding at the starboard or the windward end of the line have also been tried. The simplest procedure is to tilt the line so that the port end is slightly advantageous. Thus in the illustration, boats starting on port tack could expect to cross those starting on starboard. Fig. 12.

The favouring of one end of the line often occurs even without the wish of the sailing committee if there is a shift of wind shortly before the start. So it is as well to make a trial trip on each tack shortly before the start to make sure which is going to suit better for the first mark.

Any distance gained by starting at one end of the line rather than the other will be worth more in terms of minutes and seconds if the current is unfavourable than it would be if the current were fair.

This is often overlooked but is important when one has to judge one's chance of crossing ahead of a herd of starboard tack boats when on port tack oneself.

Some helmsmen even prefer to start late right at the starboard end of the line rather than on the gun but not quite so far to windward. In this case, where both ends of the line are surrounded by navigable water, the usual technique for a boat starting at the starboard end is to go over on to port tack as quickly as possible after the start in order to keep clear of wind and water disturbed by other boats.

If you are not in the lead, this technique also ensures that you can complete your vulnerable first port tack without interference from starboard tack boats.

Some race committees use a different method of avoiding a scrum at the starboard end of the line. They add a rider to the sailing instructions disqualifying any boat which is over the starting line or its extension after the five-minute gun.

7. Enterprises rounding a mark at Brancaster Staithe during the Schools National Championships. 8670 has been able to round before 12176 by virtue of an overlap established prior to arriving within two boat lengths of the mark; but the latter boat has tacked pretty smartly to cover.

8. All the thrill of dinghy racing is summed up in this picture but it is seldom that you can enjoy this kind of performance without the risk of a capsize.

This is popular with the sailing committees that have to start the races but not so popular with the starters themselves. In the first place it adds to the difficulties of timing and excludes various otherwise legitimate starts made by crossing the starting line from the wrong side just before the gun—a practice particularly useful on days when there is a strong current setting boats away behind the line. Therefore experiments have been tried in which the penalty period has been reduced to two minutes or even one. And those over the line during the penalty period are not disqualified if they return by crossing the extension of the starting line as opposed to the line itself. Even so it's sometimes a golden rule not to fight too hard for either end of the line.

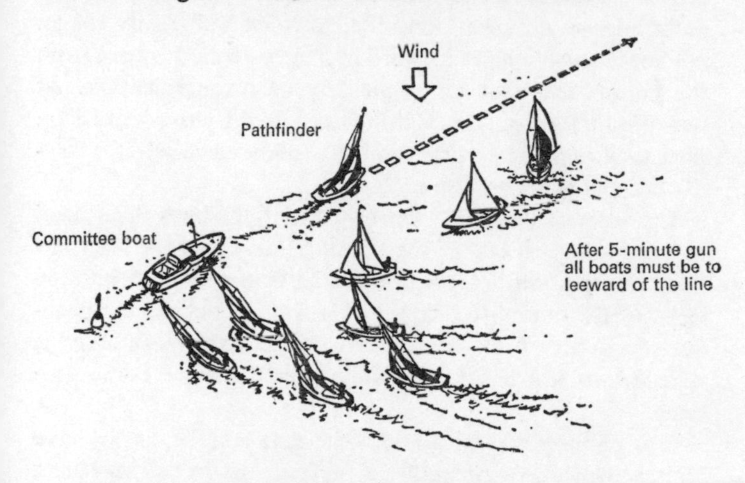

FIG. 13. The Gate Start. The starting line is set by a Pathfinder sailing a close-hauled course from the Committee Boat, setting off 2 minutes before the starting signal. 10 seconds before the starting gun, a buoy is dropped from the Committee Boat to mark the port end of the starting line. When the starting gun is fired, the Committee Boat follows the Pathfinder, and all yachts must cross the starting line astern of the Committee Boat.

The Gate Start is another system used to avoid crowding at one end of the line. In this case the starting line is set by a boat sailing close hauled on port tack starting from a mark dropped by the committee vessel. Any boat is free to sail across the line astern of this close-hauled boat, or to be more accurate, of the committee vessel which is immediately following it. Those who start when the line is still short gain in time but those who start later gain the distance which the 'pathfinder' boat has in the meantime travelled to windward. Fig. 13.

At the five-minute gun, the committee boat will be at the spot chosen for the beginning of the windward leg of the course pointing towards a close-hauled course, and the pathfinder is moored alongside, sails set and ready to go. All boats must keep to leeward of a close-hauled course from the committee boat under penalty of disqualification. At two minutes to go the pathfinder sails off close-hauled on port tack and the committee boat follows behind still towing the buoy.

Ten seconds before the starting signal, the buoy is released to mark the port end of the starting line. Once the start has been signalled all boats may cross between the mark and the stern of the committee vessel as it follows behind the pathfinder dinghy. After about two minutes the pathfinder is released to make his own start astern of the committee boat.

One of the difficulties about the gate start is, as we have seen, that if everyone makes a perfect start in this way then the chances are that they will all arrive at the first mark at about the same moment.

Another difficulty is that if the pathfinder is an ace helmsman then everybody will gain by starting at the late end of the line and the temptation will be to make a barging start there. (This may happen anyway if the committee boat stops before the starters are expecting it to do so.) On the other hand if, as is more likely, the pathfinder helmsman is only moderate everyone will try to start at the early end of the line and there will be overcrowding there too.

It is important to sense in good time if there is any danger of a premature start. The later you leave it the more boats you will have to avoid on your way back.

If you *are* over the line at the start you lose your normal rights while getting into position to restart but retain them nevertheless until it is clear that you *are* indeed returning to start. Needless to say the sooner you do return the better.

But I am quite certain of this; that in any starting system however perfect only about one in twenty of the starters will be absolutely satisfied with their getaway.

9

Racing Techniques

During those first few minutes after the start you will be sailing level with the top helmsmen in the field, the ones who will probably take the leading places at the finish. How do they do it time after time?

Certainly a well-tuned boat helps—and the experience of previous races—a sense of direction and balance—a sense of judgement too, and a faculty for observing and reacting quickly. But more than all these is needed—concentration. Concentration saves you from getting flustered after a poor start and when a speed-boat knocks all the wind out of your sails. A helmsman probably loses far more by allowing such misfortunes to disturb his concentration than he does from the mishap itself.

In our changeable climate the wind is often lighter than one had hoped for, or stronger than one needs. Certainly the extreme days—light or heavy—impress themselves more deeply on the memory than any others. And each extreme requires a different technique no matter what boat is being sailed.

When the clouds are scudding and the wind howls I believe in allowing more time than usual for getting the boat ready. This is because in a high wind there is always a greater likelihood of something snarling up or blowing away and when sails flap around like the flippers of a giant skate and ropes writhe like snakes around one's head, everything takes longer.

Apart from checking and double-checking that all is free (except what has to be made fast), the main thing to remember is that the sails should in general be pulled out really hard on the foot and luff in heavy weather in order to flatten them so that they can spill all the wind you want to spill.

For the same reason it is important to get the kicking strap tight, since the boat is far more easily controlled during a gybe if the sail is flat than if it is curvaceous and liable to fill unexpectedly with wind.

Next, at the start, allow yourself more room. Most boats are not so well under control on heavy days. They heel more, and when this happens unexpectedly a tangle of masts may result. Also every boat moves at twice its normal speed and you may not notice one approaching; sometimes a high wind may smother a warning hail. Buoys bob and weave about more; give them an extra wide berth. At the start the starboard tack is more valuable than ever. Tacking is harder and often slower on a rough day, so it is as well to allow extra time for going about in order to avoid a right-of-way boat.

When manœuvring before the start it may pay to have the centre-plate about half up; if the plate is fully down it may be difficult to bear away at a moment's notice, as you may have to in order to keep out of trouble. It is surprising how devastating the effect can be when the plate is an inch or two too far up or too far down in a 20-knot breeze. Planing in heavy weather is an art in itself.

The helmsman who can get his boat to plane a few seconds ahead of the other boats can gain hundreds of yards in the right weather. To plane smoothly the boat must be kept on a level. One way of doing this is to bear off slightly as soon as the planing gust hits you. This avoids heeling and exploits the wind's new energy at once. Then, as the apparent wind

THE BEAUFORT WIND SCALE					
Beaufort No.	Wind	Speed in knots	Weather map symbol	State of the sea	Sailing Conditions
0 1	Calm Light air	0 - 1 1 - 3		mirror-like ripples	becalmed. steerage way
2	Light breeze	4 - 6		small wavelets	likely speed 1 to 3 knots
3	Gentle breeze	7 - 10		large wavelets, crests begin to break	likely speed 4 to 6 knots
4	Moderate breeze	11 - 16		small waves, some whitecrests	likely speed 7 to 10 knots
5	Fresh breeze	17 - 21		moderate, longer waves, many 'white horses' & some spray.	good sailing weather but wear oilskins
6	Strong breeze	22 - 27		large waves form. many whitecrests more spray	shorten sail
7	Moderate gale	28 - 33		sea banks up streaks of foam. some spindrift	small boats stay in port, large boats reef down
8	Fresh gale	34 - 40		fairly high waves, spindrift & streaks of foam	all boats better in harbour
9	Strong gale	41 - 47		steep waves, foam and spray affect visibility	perilous at sea
10	Whole gale	48 - 55		very large waves with overhanging crests, big patches of foam, sea white, visibility reduced	
11	Storm	56 - 66		extra big seas, much foam, crests become froth, visibility poor	
12	Hurricane	over 66		seas huge & white, air filled with foam, driving spray, visibility very poor	

FIG. 14.

goes ahead with the boat's extra speed you sheet in and point up again on to your fastest course.

If the boat is reaching across a succession of seas, try to ride the waves by planing along the crests, and since the crests are moving forward the boat will have to be pointed not parallel to the line of waves but slightly forward of this.

Some people are happy to pull the centre-board right up when planing and say that it 'helps to keep the hull under the mast'. But some lowered plate helps to avoid rolling. This is something you must discover for yourself.

If a boat heels during a plane and the stem is forced into a wave on a slant instead of upright, the water, acting on the uneven angled side of the hull may force a sudden change of course leading perhaps to a capsize. Therefore, in small boats that plane, it is generally safer to keep the weight well aft so that the boat rests on the flat after-sections and thus ensure that she is kept level.

Plenty of practice is the best way of facing up to heavy weather. One of the hardest problems is to get sufficient new experience without sailing on days when racing would be foolhardy. You have to push yourself to the limit but not beyond. I mentioned various emergencies that can occur in heavy weather—including a capsize and ways of dealing in an earlier book entitled *Starting to Sail.*

Anyone who races should also read a small book called *Water Wisdom* by E. F. Haylock published by the British Petroleum Company for the Royal Yachting Association, price 5/-. Its object is to show 'how to have fun afloat safely' and to avoid accidents. There is so much more to the game than buoyancy tests, knowing man-overboard drill and being able to right a capsized dinghy by standing on the centre-plate and getting the mainsail down (and remembering *not* to leave the boat under the mistaken impression that you can swim ashore).

This book covers subjects such as ocean racing, rescue services available (and how to alert them—you can now get 'personal' distress signals), towing at sea, and first aid. It also lists makers of approved life-jackets (which give complete body support) and buoyancy aids (for inshore racing).

And these words are golden advice to rescuers and rescued. '*Cold Water—Get out of it*' Man is a warm blooded animal. Maintenance of body temperature is an important and delicate process. If he falls into cold water he soon begins to lose the ability to help himself, to hold on to a lifebuoy or boat for instance. Get him out of it quickly. He may seem cheerful and even wave to his would-be rescuers. Within minutes he has gone. The colder the water the quicker this happens. His life-jacket will not save him from this hazard.

The sea around Britain is cold offshore until well on in the year. Even then it is still pretty cold.

Having got out of the sea, never, never stand around in wet clothes in cold winds or, for that matter, in any wind. Get dry and get into dry clothes. The chill caused by evaporation can be as potent a killer as the cold sea.

If unable to change into dry clothes immediately, put on a windproof garment such as an oilskin and, if possible, shelter from the wind.

Lakes and rivers which may be fed by mountain streams are often very cold. This also applies to flooded gravel pits. 'Frostbite sailors—be warned!'

In most races it is sound practice to include in the sailing instructions a provision to disqualify any boat which capsizes to the point where its racing flag touches the water. But for this rule there would be a temptation for the helmsman and crew to right the boat and carry on racing in a waterlogged unseaworthy condition and rescue boats might have to approach the same boat two or three times without being allowed to offer assistance.

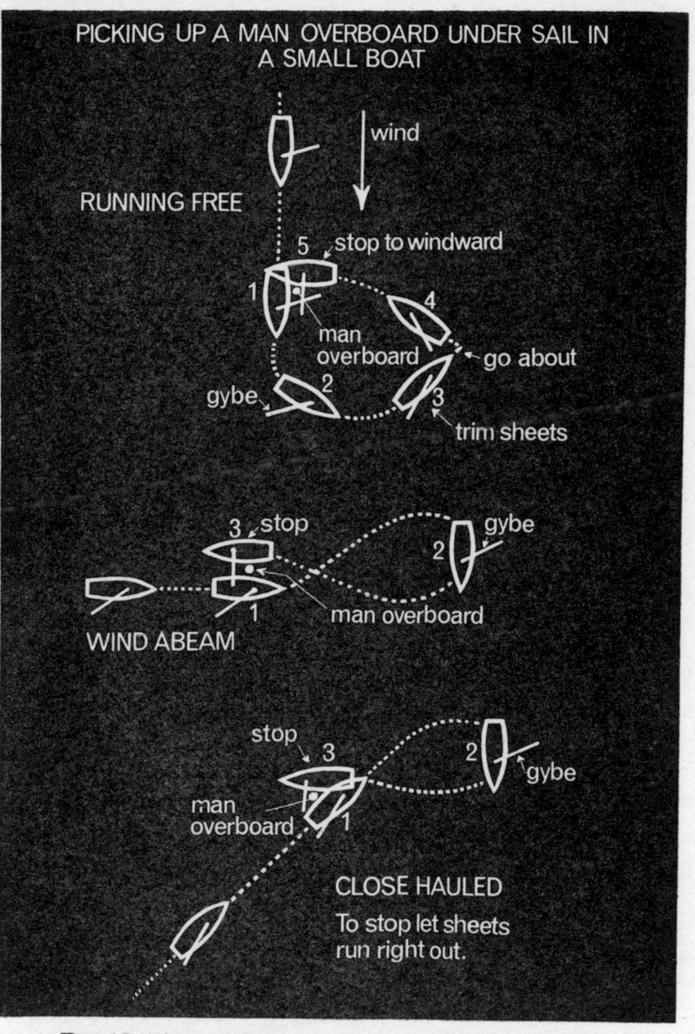

FIG. 15. This covers most cases, but remember in some boats it is easier to come aboard over the transom than over the side, and to keep boat stationary and under control, back the jib and trim the mainsheet slightly to compensate.

The chief problem in light weather is very different. It is to continue concentrating on the race—which is all the longer for its slow speed—at a time when the boat sails herself and the weather encourages one to laze—even to sunbathe.

The extra concentration is needed because on light days, two boats less than fifty yards apart may have winds of quite different strength and direction. The helmsman who knows how to perceive and make use of these slight variations is the one who comes home first.

When the wind changes round say from north or some other direction to south as often happens on a south coast for example when the sea-breeze comes in there are frequently dead patches. So if you are in the old breeze stay with it as long as it will stay with you, even if it takes you a little off course.

A strand or two of black wool or thread tied to each shroud may help you to see which way the wind blows.

A full cut sail pays dividends on a light day because it produces greater power and yet the heeling effect is within the capabilities of the crew to counteract.

On light days use the lightest tackle and sheets that you can safely fit and see that all blocks run smoothly. Full sails which catch the wind are a help in light airs and as already mentioned it may be useful to carry a kedge to stop the boat being driven astern by the current when there is too little wind to stem it.

It takes much longer on a light day for the boat to pick up speed than when there is plenty of wind. Therefore never let the boat stop if you can possibly help it particularly just before the start. Sometimes the to-and-fro movement of boats near the starting line will send a light wind up towards the stratosphere and if one once falls into this dead patch without enough way to get through it the result can be disastrous. Moreover even a small wave can take quite a lot of speed off a small boat when there is little wind; these waves tend to build up just before the start because the boats are at close quarters and because they are turning in small circles.

Keep the boat moving, without rocking her too much. Every movement of the rudder or of the centre-plate acts to some extent as a brake. It usually pays to keep close to the line, provided that the boat continues to move with full way on her.

Trim the boat to reduce her wetted surface as much as possible. In many small planing boats it pays to get well forward in light airs because even a slight forward tilt will lift a considerable area of the flat after sections of the hull out of the water.

Sometimes it may be necessary to heel the boat slightly to leeward in order to keep the sails full and for the same reason when tacking the helmsman sometimes finds that it pays not to change sides until after the boom has come across to the new leeward side. When beating to windward on light days one has to sail somewhat freer because at fine angles a light wind has not enough punch to get the boat moving at her best.

Of course if there is any current a new factor comes into play. If the current is running towards the first mark one must stay well back from the starting line to avoid getting carried over—a calamity which can easily happen if the wind drops for a few seconds. And if the current is foul, you may, if the sailing instructions allow it, stay the wrong side of the line and recross it just before the starting signal has been made in order to make a normal start.

There are a number of general principles for making the best use of the current, these are:

1. The current generally runs more strongly in the middle

of the mainstream than at the edges. This also applies to river currents.

2. The current usually runs fastest in the middle part of the period of tidal ebb or flow, but this depends to some extent on local conditions such as the coastline and the changing shape of a channel at various stages of high or low water. The behaviour of the current does not always correspond to the predicted rise or fall of the level of the water, and it is better if possible to establish this from observation of the flow of the water past obstacles such as buoys, than to rely on tide tables.

3. A current tends to sweep outwards on a bend.

4. It also runs faster in sections where the channel narrows or where there is an isolated spit or shallow. On the down current side of such an obstacle there is often an eddy or an area of still water—indicated by floating driftwood etc.

5. The current tends to change direction first at the edges of the tidal stream.

When plugging up an estuary against the current it is best, other things being equal, to choose the side which has fewer tributaries pouring into it. Fig. 16.

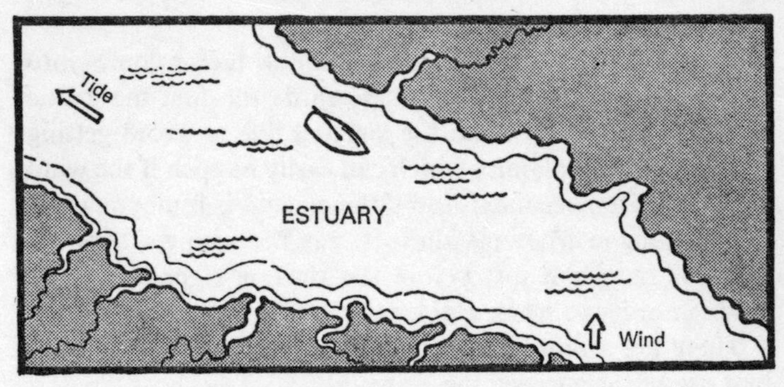

FIG. 16. When plugging up an estuary, take the side with the fewest tributaries.

When beating against the current always look for the possibility of getting it to act on the lee bow of the boat, in which case she will be pushed up to windward. In certain circumstances an adverse current will push you to windward if the boat is pinched but not if she is sailed on a normal close-hauled course.

When working against the current remember that only a very slight drop in speed may halve your rate of progress over the ground because your surplus of speed over the ground has already been greatly reduced.

FIG. 17. In a tideway, look for the possibility of lee-bowing the tide as this yacht is doing.

If you have to cross the main stream of an adverse current, travel at good speed and avoid pinching. When you have been hugging the shore to avoid the current and have to leave it to round a mark, you should, if you are leading a boat, plan to come out into the stream about the same time as the following boat unless she is a long way behind in which case you can choose your own moment.

And if you expect the wind to drop during the race get well up-tide during the early stages while there is still enough breeze to take you there.

When beating the golden rule is to concentrate on speed first and then direction. Speed allows you to steer accurately and go about smartly on to the other tack when the wind

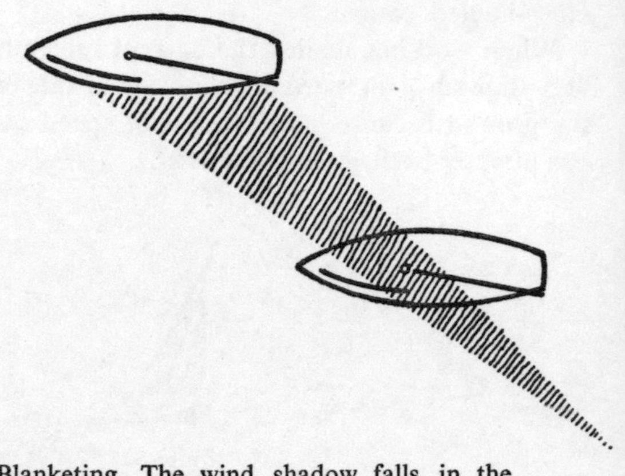

FIG. 18. Blanketing. The wind shadow falls in the direction of the apparent wind and not the true wind.

heads you. And once you have got the boat really travelling you will begin to feel what I can only describe as a kind of 'rhythmic balanced progress' during which you flip from one tack to the other like a swallow flitting across a meadow. And if you don't get a glimmering of this feeling when beating, you can be certain that the boat is not really travelling.

Sail your own race. That is, if you've decided to keep to the 'starboard shore'—the one you can sail off on starboard tack—don't allow yourself to be driven away from it by starboard tack boats. Cross astern of them if need be.

Here are a few more well-tried hints.

If there is one long and one short tack to the mark, take the long tack first because you are almost always bound to benefit more if there is a windshift on the way.

Unless the direction of the wind and that of the seas is the same, one tack will mean more slogging into the waves than the other and when on this tack you will have to bear away and sail freer in order to keep the boat moving.

The forefoot of the boat should be well into the water to make the boat sail on its full designed water-line length.

The jib should not be in too hard in light weather, when you want to sail a little freer, or when the boat has to be kept moving in a sea-way.

The quickest way of spilling unwanted wind in a dinghy, and so keeping the boat level, which is how she should be, is to let out some mainsheet. It's a pity to have to do this but sitting out further to get her level brings slower results (and scarcely any result at all if the boat is already heeling) and a small boat may get stopped if one tries to spill wind by luffing up.

When beating to windward in a race it is not enough to see that the boat moves her fastest, points her best and lays the mark without unneeded tacks. There is also the problem of how to hinder other boats.

For example if one boat is ahead and to windward of another, her wind shadow will prevent the other boat from sailing at full speed. Therefore it is often profitable to tack into a position which gives you this safe windward position as it is called since this may force the other boat to put in two extra tacks to get a clear wind. Sometimes the other boat, because of the shore, may not be able to tack clear in which case the manœuvre is better still.

The wind shadow of a boat falls in the direction of the apparent wind and not the true wind. Fig. 18.

If you are specially interested in staying ahead of one particular boat it may pay to try for the safe windward position and cover her on each tack as she goes about. On the other hand it often happens that while you are concen-

FIG. 19. The leading boat is in what is known as the 'safe leeward position', but cannot round the mark without tacking in her opponent's water.

trating on this one boat, several others, who are able to sail any course they please, slip through. And if there are two possible courses to the next mark and you want the boat behind to follow you it is as well not to cover her too rigidly.

If when approaching a boat on the opposite tack, it becomes clear that you are not going to have time to cross ahead of her and tack into the safe windward position, you may be able to get into the safe leeward position. In this, your boat is well ahead but slightly to leeward of the other boat and the deflected wind from your own sails interferes with the supply of wind to the other boat.

Once in the safe leeward position it may be possible to pinch up to windward and arrive directly ahead of the following boat because her speed will have been reduced by being back-winded. The safe leeward position pays well along a windward shore which prevents the windward boat from tacking to get clear but it does not always pay when approaching a mark that requires a tack to round it as

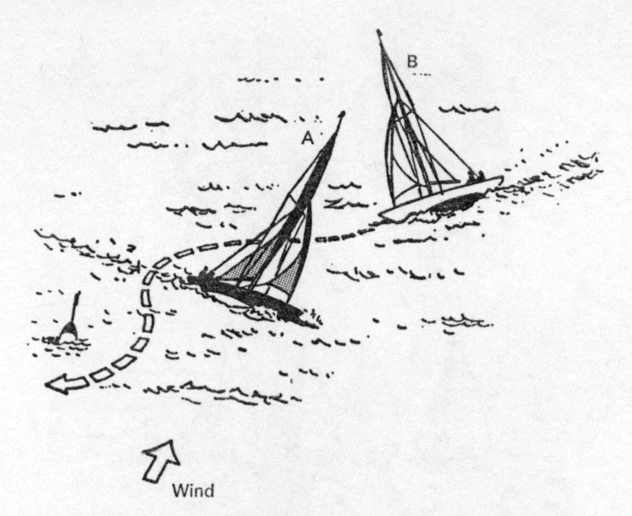

FIG. 20. On opposite tacks at the mark, although A is on the starboard tack she will drop a place at the mark because she cannot tack in B's water.

there may not be room to tack clear ahead of the following boat. When rounding a mark it is just as much a breach of the rules to obstruct a boat by tacking or gybing too close ahead of her as it would be if there were no mark. Fig. 19.

Therefore if a mark at the end of a beat has to be left to starboard, the boat which approaches it on the port tack can sometimes beat a starboard tack boat by letting her cross just ahead, after which she will be unable to take the inside position. Fig. 20.

This tactic may not work, of course, in a big race where the odds are that there will be several starboard tack boats approaching the mark at the same time. It is even more risky if the windward mark has to be left to port since the port tack boat herself will have to tack in order to round it.

When rounding the mark it is important to carry in your

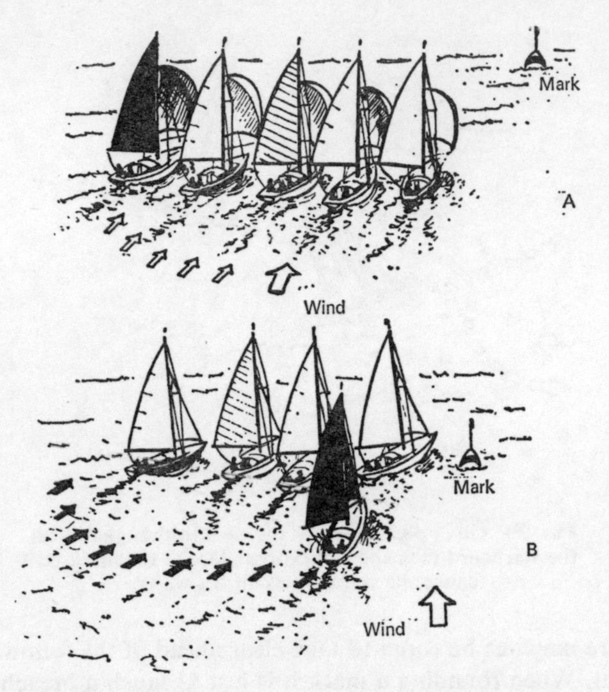

FIG. 21. When running level as the mark is approached (A), the leeward boat drops back (B), then moves across up-wind behind the windward boat, but ahead of the rest. She must be careful, however, not to barge in if the first yacht forges ahead.

mind's eye the picture of the situation as it will be after rounding.

For example if you are running level with several other boats towards the end of a down-wind leg, it is often worth dropping several places temporarily in order to get an inside berth at the mark if this leaves you to windward after rounding. Fig. 21.

If the leeward mark is not overcrowded and the next mark

is to windward, it pays to keep well away from the mark on the arrival side so that it can be rounded closely on the departure side. A boat that follows this course gains ground to windward over a boat that makes a close approach to the buoy.

When rounding a mark at high speed at the end of a reach or run don't forget to allow for the fact that the mast will tend to swing outwards during the turn and the crew and helmsman therefore may have to sit out during the manœuvre.

No doubt at some time you will be asked to handle a spinnaker and you will find the arrangements vary according to the size of boat, the cut of the sail and the preferences of the helmsman. In 12-metre boats they have a system in which the spinnaker pole is never removed from the mast but is dipped under the fore-stay when the spinnaker has to be gybed. Also, by allowing either the port or the starboard after-guy (the after guy is wire rope that prevents the spinnaker boom from swinging forwards) to run loosely through the end of the pole on its way to the sail 12-metre crews avoid having to do any clipping or un-clipping during a gybe.

But it still takes eleven men to do a gybe, which means continuous practice. And even setting or taking in a large spinnaker can be an epic occasion. The need for spinnaker drill is however just as great on small boats as on large.

In theory the spinnaker boom should always be kept at right angles to the wind whilst the sheet (the rope holding the corner of the spinnaker that is not attached to the spinnaker boom) has to be trimmed accordingly. And since the true direction of the wind usually varies to some extent with the speed of the boat, and thus the apparent wind varies as well, there is never a dull moment on the run.

A boat running directly before the wind sails more slowly

than one on a broad reach and for this reason many helmsmen believe in sailing a zigzag course on a run changing at intervals from one gybe to another. Only experience can show how your boat responds to this technique, but remember in travelling with the current your deviations from a straight course will be lessened whereas with the current against you they will be correspondingly exaggerated. Downwind tacking probably pays better when the wind is light than when it is blowing hard.

When finishing remember that the shortest course to the line is not always the quickest. It may be quicker to cross the line further to leeward or windward if you can get there on a 'plane'.

10

Keeping the Score

If every race were a complete contest in itself there would be no difficulty about keeping the score. One would simply record the order in which the boats finished on that particular day.

But not every race is important enough to carry a prize and so the system has grown up by which the award goes to the boat with the best performance over a series of races lasting perhaps over a week-end, or a week, or even over the season. The placings are determined according to the total number of points earned by each yacht during the series of races.

And this is where the difficulty lies, for the number of starters is liable to vary from race to race. The problem is to decide how much more, if any, a boat should earn for winning a race in which there are, say, twelve starters than she should for winning when the field is only seven.

Any system that gives the winning boat the same number of points irrespective of the size of the fleet gives an unreasonable bonus to boats winning in small turnouts and is therefore unfair to the absentees on days when a large proportion of the class fails to start.

But any system which cuts the number of points awarded to competitors in a reduced fleet can be equally unfair to starters who may be sailing just as well that day as on any other. No system that I know has entirely overcome this difficulty.

KEEPING THE SCORE

Points For Races

Starters

Place	2	3	4	5	6	7	8	9	10	11	12	13	14	15	16	17	18	19	20	Place
1st	3	4	5	5	6	7	7	8	9	9	10	11	11	12	13	13	14	15	15	1st
2nd	1	2	3	3	4	5	5	6	7	7	8	9	9	10	11	11	12	13	13	2nd
3rd		1	2	2	3	4	4	5	6	6	7	8	8	9	10	10	11	12	12	3rd
4th			1	1	2	3	3	4	5	5	6	7	7	8	9	9	10	11	11	4th
5th				1	1	2	2	3	4	4	5	6	6	7	8	8	9	10	10	5th
6th					1	1	1	2	3	3	4	5	5	6	7	7	8	9	9	6th
7th						1	1	1	2	2	3	4	4	5	6	6	7	8	8	7th
8th							1	1	1	1	2	3	3	4	5	5	6	7	7	8th
9th								1	1	1	1	2	2	3	4	4	5	6	6	9th
10th									1	1	1	1	1	2	3	3	4	5	5	10th
11th										1	1	1	1	1	2	2	3	4	4	11th
12th											1	1	1	1	1	1	2	3	3	12th
13th												1	1	1	1	1	1	2	2	13th
14th													1	1	1	1	1	1	1	14th
15th														1	1	1	1	1	1	15th
16th															1	1	1	1	1	16th
17th																1	1	1	1	17th
18th																	1	1	1	18th
19th																		1	1	19th
20th																			1	20th

Some clubs use an average system. One version of which totals the points scored by a boat during the season and divides this by the number of races in which she took part. The object of this is to put the boat whose owner cannot race regularly on the same footing as the man who lives on the spot and can therefore be certain of racing each week-end. The drawback to the averaging system, however, is that, if a man is 'points conscious,' he may be discouraged from turning out in small fields which would lower his average score even if he won.

A simple table which avoids averaging and involves no higher mathematics is set out on the opposite page.

The points are graded to make even small turnouts worth while; it is assumed that there is not much to choose between the more backward boats in a large fleet.

The International Snipe Class Racing Association has put forward a system to allow competition between Snipe owners of different clubs even though these clubs do not actually race against one another. In this system points are awarded to the boats according to the order in which they finish, irrespective of the number of boats in the race. (This is to avoid the clubs with larger fleets having a permanent advantage.) However, for a race to be valid, at least five boats must take part and the course must be 2½ miles long. In order to equalize things as between clubs with a long racing season and those with a short one the scores are averaged. But the assumption is made that it should be possible to race at least fifteen times in a season and bonus points can be added to each boat's score for each race sailed up to a total of fifteen races.

Another method of scoring devised to ensure maximum turnouts is known as the Low Point system. In one version of the Low Point system the first boat home scores zero, the second one and so on. This is known as a 'linear' system because a graph obtained by plotting points awarded against places gained gives a straight line. At the end of the season the total number of points scored by each boat is divided by the number of races sailed to give her final rating. Under this system however a boat cannot improve her average by staying out of a race, for all boats not racing are automatically scored as if they had finished in the class.

It is true that under this low point system you gain no more by beating dozens of boats than you do for coming in ahead of the only other starter. Yet it can be argued that beating a large number of indifferent helmsmen is not what counts. It is getting ahead of those really good ones in the front of the fleet that is important.

Incidentally the low point scoring system has another advantage. It allows you to compare easily one year's performance with another.

The new Olympic Games scoring system adopted by the International Yacht Racing Union is a low point system which gives a graduated premium to the six leading boats (though not so heavy as under the previous system).

In this the	First boat scores	0
	Second boat	3
	Third boat	5.7
	Fourth boat	8
	Fifth boat	10
	Sixth boat	11.7
	Seventh boat	place plus 6
	and so on...	

The full text of the Olympic system including the arrangements for non-finishers, tie-breaking, etc., is obtainable from the IYRU or the RYA.

This arrangement gives the leading boats a 'bonus' which they do not have under the linear form of low point scoring described above. It also avoids over-penalizing the man who has one bad race in an otherwise good series.

For example, in the linear system, a boat finishing twentieth in a field of twenty loses 10 points to a boat finishing tenth, and next day, assuming that the other boat was again tenth, he would have to win to keep the score level. Under the Olympics system, he could gain back the same 10 points by coming home in third place.

Finally there is the refinement of 'dropped' races. For example in a series of points races lasting over the whole season of say thirty weeks it would be unreasonable to expect everyone to be able to take part in every race. Equally it might discourage helmsmen from racing to the full if the contest were limited to say twelve specific dates or even to the first twelve races sailed by any given owner. Averaging also has its disadvantages. But if the owner is allowed to pick the best twelve races from any number which he sails (and drops the others), then the racing conditions are more nearly levelled up. This then is the system adopted by many clubs.

In some class championships each helmsman is allowed to drop one race during the week for the purpose of the week's points championship, so that if, for example, five races are sailed, only the competitor's best four count.

There are arguments for and against this practice. There are circumstances of course when a helmsman may have genuine misfortune at the start or through a wind-shift. In such cases it would seem only just to allow a race to be dropped.

On the other hand it has been argued that if a helmsman reaches the last race in a series without having had to drop a race, he may, having something in hand, feel that he can sail closer to other boats than he might otherwise do and even risk a collision since a disqualification will not reduce the total he has scored already.

It is just possible that a thought of this kind might influence a helmsman in his judgement of a borderline case. However, if he is already in a strong enough position to be able to risk throwing away a race, then he may well have no need of the points which he could gain by taking that risk. And it seems just as likely that a helmsman who has already mishandled a race and needs a first place to recover his position will take a 'win-all, lose-all' risk.

One needs to be a thought reader or a psychiatrist to be certain.

The Olympic system is to hold seven races for each class of which each competitor's best six are counted.

If there is a tie on total points the yacht with the most 1st places wins or if this doesn't settle matters the yacht with the most second places and so on. If this method fails in respect of the six races sailed, the series is considered tied. The discarded race is disregarded.

If there is a dead heat in an individual race the total of points for 1st and 2nd places are divided equally between the two boats concerned. If a yacht's finishing position is prejudiced through assisting another yacht in distress or through a foul by another yacht she is given points equal to the average of her five best races.

The Olympics penalty for not retiring after a breach of the rules is to score for a last place finish plus 10 per cent of the number of yachts starting in the race. Any fractions are raised to the next highest whole number.

11

Protests and Appeals

You might conclude from the fact that this small book contains a section on protests and appeals that they often occur. This is not the case except perhaps among comparative beginners who have not fully understood the rules or how to apply them.

Experienced helmsmen usually anticipate and avoid situations which might invite protests against them, and if, as sometimes happens, they misjudge things then they retire without more ado.

This should be the rule for everyone who gets involved in an incident leading to a protest against which there is no adequate defence.

However if a club has no protests it can mean that the helmsmen who sail there are not experienced but, on the contrary, too easy going. Sometimes, although two yachts have come into collision, neither protests. To avoid this one well-known club insists, in its permanent sailing instructions, on a protest being brought if one of two yachts in a collision does not retire. Under this rule, failure to protest in the proper manner can lead to the disqualification of *both* yachts. One day this rule may be adopted internationally.

There is nothing unsporting about making a protest or in contesting it in good faith or appealing to the RYA against the Sailing Committee's decision.

The whole protest system is devised to make up for the fact that, as yacht races take place often on the open sea and not on a severely limited sports ground, it is impossible to have a referee on the spot ready to whistle 'offside' or to award a penalty. Consequently an 'inquest' has to be held afterwards.

If a helmsman thinks that he has been unfairly treated by another competitor it is far better that he should formally protest so that his evidence can be heard and, if necessary, contested than that he should wander about nursing a grievance and perhaps even unintentionally maligning someone without giving him a chance to defend himself. Also, if you don't bring a protest, the insurance company may want to know why before they pay for any damage sustained in a collision.

Finally, protests are often extremely useful in helping to interpret the rules of sailing, in cutting out loopholes and uncertainties in the wording—and in some cases in making progress towards the, as yet non-existent, perfect rule.

A protest can be made by any competitor against another and if the protest occurs between yachts competing in separate races sponsored by different clubs the case is heard by a combined committee of both clubs.

A helmsman who wishes to protest must do his best to tell the other yacht that a protest will be lodged. This is only fair because the 'accused' then has as good a chance of remembering the circumstances of the case as the helmsman who is making the protest.

For this reason a protest flag has to be flown conspicuously in the rigging at the first reasonable opportunity and must be kept flying until the protester has finished his race (also as a warning to the officer of the day) unless the competitor's boat was dismasted, capsized, or sunk, or unless he did not know the facts justifying the protest until later. Even in this case, however, the protesting helmsman must make an effort to find and warn the other yachtsmen concerned. The protest flag must be either a flag or a burgee or a rectangular piece of material no smaller than the distinguishing flag usually flown by the protesting yacht. In the case of a yacht being sailed single-handed it might be difficult for the helmsman with only one pair of hands to hoist a protest flag, so it is considered enough if the flag is brought to the notice of the other helmsman (for example, by waving it) as soon as possible after the incident and to the committee when the finishing line is crossed at the finish. If a yacht fails to observe this rule the Race Committee must refuse to accept the protest but they may still bring one on their own initiative under certain circumstances.

The Race Committee can stage a protest hearing against a helmsman if they see an apparent infringement of any rule or get a report of it from a witness who was not competing in the race or was not an interested party. They can even do so if they have reasonable grounds for supposing from the evidence at the hearing of a protest that a yacht may have committed some breach of the rules. In this case they must give notice by delivering or by posting to the helmsman involved not later than one day after the finish of the race, or of the receipt of the report, or of the hearing of the protest.

If the yacht fails to cross *the starting or finishing line* in accordance with the rules and the sailing instructions the Race Committee can disqualify the yacht without protest or hearing. A yacht penalized in this way must be told either by letter or by a note included in the official racing results. But it is open to any helmsman to protest against the Race Committee and he would presumably do so at once if they did not give him the normal finishing gun or signal if he felt aggrieved.

All protests must be in writing and must state: the date, time, and whereabouts of the incidents; the rule or rules or sailing instructions alleged to have been broken or infringed; a description of the incident and if necessary a diagram showing the course, position, and tracks of the vessels, and the direction and strength of the wind and tide and the depth of water if relevant. The printed protest forms which can be got from the RYA save a great deal of trouble to anyone who is not already sure how to present a protest.

The protest must be signed by the owner or his representative and lodged or, if that is impossible, posted within two hours of the finish of the protesting yacht or, should she not finish, within two hours of her arrival at an anchorage or within such special time limit and with such fee, if any, as may have been prescribed in the sailing directions.

These regulations are planned to discourage frivolous or unreasonably vague protests which would waste the time of the Race Committee and of everyone else concerned.

It will be noticed that the Race Committee may extend the time. This is just as well if, for example, the anchorage happens to be twenty miles or so by road from the club, and the helmsman who has put in there for repairs after a collision has no motor transport with him.

Many sailing instructions, however, give only half an hour's grace for a protest, which can mean hard work for a helmsman who has to stow gear and sails, get ashore and then perhaps write a document while damp and dripping in the changing room. And in the meantime he has probably had to make every effort firstly, to inform the other helmsman of the protest—in case he has not seen the protest flag, and secondly, to see if he is willing to retire by not signing his declaration.

As soon as the Race Committee receive a protest they must tell the owner of the yacht protested against (or his representative) that a protest has been made and provide all parties with a copy of the protest, the time and place of hearing which should be as soon as possible provided that this allows reasonable time for a defence to be prepared.

The owner of a yacht involved in a protest or anyone chosen by him as his representative has the right to be present while the Race Committee takes the evidence, even though he may not have witnessed the incident or have been present at it, but this privilege is not extended to other witnesses.

A written protest, once made, cannot be withdrawn, but if either of the interested parties or a representative fail to make an effort to attend the hearing, the Race Committee may be justified in dismissing the case or in deciding the protest as they think fit, subject to appeal to the RYA or other body competent to hear appeals.

The decisions of the Race Committee are to be given to the parties concerned in writing if requested. The 'verdict' must include the facts found by the Race Committee and the reason for their decision.

Where there is doubt as to what actually happened during the incident owing to a conflict of evidence or for some other reason the Race Committee is entitled to determine the facts and their decision on facts, as distinct from law, is final. Even the best of helmsmen can be mistaken about what actually happened during an incident, as camera photos showed in a recent Olympic Games series, and often the truth can be arrived at only through circumstantial evidence brought out by the Race Committee.

For example if there is doubt as to whether one boat had made an overlap over another less than two lengths from an obstacle, the Race Committee, knowing the local geography, weather conditions, etc., is obviously in the best position to decide what happened. But the Race Committee's finding of fact must not of course be inconsistent with the evidence they have heard and accepted.

Equally the Race Committee's decision on law must agree with their finding of fact and must not be based on a rule that does not apply to the case.

Either party disagreeing with the Race Committee's decision on interpretation of the rules, as distinct from matters of fact, may ask the Race Committee within a limited period (ten days in the UK) after having received the Race Committee's decision to refer the case to the national authority (in Britain, the RYA.) The grounds for the appeal must be stated and a deposit (forfeited if the appeal fails) must be made. The Race Committee itself may appeal to the RYA for a ruling.

The RYA, when considering the appeal, is entitled to uphold or reverse the Race Committee's decision and if it thinks, from the facts found by the Sailing Committee, that a yacht involved in a protest has broken a rule which is applicable, then it may disqualify her irrespective of whether the incident or rule concerned was mentioned in the protest.

The Race Committee must forward the appeal to the RYA within two months of receiving it, and include with it a copy of the advertised conditions of the race and the sailing instructions; a copy of the protest or protests and all other written statements which may have been put in by the parties; the observations of the Race Committee; a full statement of the facts found; their decision and the reasons for it; an official diagram prepared by the Race Committee in accordance with the facts found by them showing (1) the course to the next mark or, if close by, the mark itself with its required side, (2) the direction and force of the wind; the set and strength of the current, if any; the depth of water if required and the positions and tracks of the yachts involved. The grounds of the appeal must be given and the observations if any by the Race Committee.

The Race Committee must also notify all parties that an

appeal is to be lodged and invite them to make any comments on it. These observations must be sent in with the appeal.

Appeals from protests can be very inconvenient in competitions or knock-out matches in which it is important to establish the results without delay and race organizers are now allowed to dispense with appeals provided that they obtain written permission in advance from the RYA and display this prominently at the time and place of the competition.

Tips on Trailers

1. Most of the expensive trailer accidents are caused by stowing extra gear in the boat and so loading the trailer with more than its designed weight.
2. Check tyre pressures and, if possible, carry a spare wheel, and jack.
3. There is a 40 m.p.h. speed limit on two-wheel trailers in Britain and other limits in certain other countries.
4. Load the trailer so that if anything it bears down slightly on the towing hitch.
5. Lights and number plate. The trailer must display rear lights, brake lights, and red reflectors. Direction indicators are also needed and if the car has the flashing type then these must be repeated on the trailer. All these can be mounted on a board together with the registration number and hung on the dinghy's rudder pintles. In any case the lights and numbers must not be mounted more than 2 ft 6 ins forward of the rearmost point of the trailer or load. The number plate must also be illuminated at night.
6. Trailers weighing more than 2 cwts must legally have brakes in Britain and mudguards must be fitted.
7. Small diameter tyres may mean easier launching (if you don't use a trolley): large diameter tyres mean a smoother ride and less wear.
8. A bumper is not a towing-bar.
9. In the U.S. many states insist on the trailer being secured to the car with safety chains in addition to the hitch.

Bibliography

Adlard Coles Ltd. publish a wide range of books on sailing. Here are a few which will interest anyone who would like to learn more about the subject.

Construction and Care of Dinghies, *Kenneth Mason and Richard Creagh-Osborne,* 12/6

Dinghy Building, *Richard Creagh-Osborne*, 50/-

Dinghy Management, *Richard Creagh-Osborne*, 6/-

The Glenans Sailing Manual, *Centre Nautique des Glenans*, 50/-

Invitation to Sailing, *Alan Brown*, 25/-

The New Small Boat Sailing, *John Fisher*, 21/-

Paul Elvström Explains the Racing Rules (in association with Richard Creagh-Osborne and Partners), 18/-

Racing Dinghy Handling, *Ian Proctor*, 21/-

Sailing: from start to finish, *Yves-Louis Pinaud*, 63/-

Sailing Theory and Practice, *C. A. Marchaj*, 105/-

Sailing: Wind and Current, *Ian Proctor*, 25/-

Wind and Sailing Boats, *Alan Watts*, 50/-

Yacht and Dinghy Racing, *Hugh Somerville*, 30/-